Let's Look at Dance!

Using Professional Dance on Video

Linda Rolfe and Mary Harlow

with photographs by Bill Cooper

David Fulton Publishers
London

David Fulton Publishers Ltd
2 Barbon Close, London WC1N 3JX

First published in Great Britain by
David Fulton Publishers Ltd 1997

Note: The right of Linda Rolfe and Mary Harlow to be identified as the authors of this work has been asserted by them in accordance with the Copyright, Designs and Patents Act, 1988.

Photographs © Bill Cooper, Gabrielle Crawford, Houston Ballet, The Royal Ballet and The Rambert Dance Company

British Library Cataloguing in Publication Data

A catalogue record for this book is available from the British Library

ISBN 1–85346–430–9

Typeset by FSH Print and Production Limited, London
Printed in Great Britain by Bell & Bain Ltd., Glasgow

Contents

Acknowledgements

We thank the following for their help:

- Bill Cooper, photographer.

- Tony Cooper, Deputy Headteacher of St Saviours Junior School, Bath, and his Year 4 children, for his continual support and guidance, trialling materials and providing the Gift of Tradition evaluation worksheet.

- Gabrielle Crawford, photographer, Late Flowering Lust.

- Andrew Edmonson, Press Office, Houston Ballet, USA.

- The Education Unit of the Royal Ballet, Royal Opera House, London.

- Jane Pritchard, Archivist for Rambert Dance Company.

- Alan Rees, Headteacher of Westbury Park Primary School, Bristol, for kindly allowing the school to be used for a photographic session.

- Dancers in the non-professional photographs: Kelly Sloan, Lysi Bunker, Lydia Robertson, Jessica Rees, Katie Buswell, Victoria Chilcott, Adrian Longdon and Rachel Robertson for generously giving their time and dance expertise.

- Julie Williams, whose skills and initiative contributed enormously to the typing of the manuscript.

Preface

Teachers of dance must celebrate and embrace the technology which now enables us to use professional dance works on video as exemplars from which children can learn to create, perform and appreciate dances. This development in dance education means that every child has the opportunity to access dance from diverse cultures and artistic traditions, including a range of dance styles which demonstrate the work of many different choreographers. As in the other arts we are now able to make reference to the world of dance as it exists in the public domain. It is by developing aesthetic awareness and artistic understanding of given dance works that children and teachers can enhance their own creativity in dance. Through opening doors into the rich panorama of dance tradition and convention now available on video, children can engage with a repertoire of dance which will inform and extend their own skills, knowledge and understanding of the art form. Their creative possibilities will be increased and teachers have a resource which is authentic, accessible and appealing to children who are already familiar with obtaining information through different visual media.

The learning potential of dance is greatly increased by watching it in performance. In addition to live performances, the video player can now bring dance into every classroom, hall or lecture theatre.

Our research has been undertaken in various teaching and learning contexts which include working with children and teachers on professional development courses and conferences across England and Wales, as well as lecturing to initial teacher training students. Our information has been collected through several methods, such as:

- Talking with children, students and teachers about the use of dance on video
- Teaching children, students and teachers through using dance on video
- Classroom observation of teachers using the material
- Written evaluations of the material from teachers and children
- National and local conference presentations on using this approach to dance in education.

Linda Rolfe and Mary Harlow
Exeter and Bristol
December 1996

Table of videos used

The following videos are described and explained fully, with dance ideas and detailed dance frameworks. Teaching points are identified and learning outcomes specified.

The following videos are referred to briefly (see pp. 82–84).

Video title	Dance context and ideas
14.Dance for the Camera – Outside In	Performed by CandoCo, a company of able-bodied and disabled dancers
15.Dancehouse	12 x 5 minute contemporary dance works
16.Dance into Schools – The Jiving Lindy Hoppers	Lindy Hop and Big Apple dance styles
17.Dein Perry's Tap Dogs	A dazzling display of tap-dancing by an all-male dance group
18.Different steps – The work of 3	Wildlife by Richard Alston
choreographers with Rambert Dance Company	Sergeant Early's Dream by Christopher Bruce Death and the Maiden by Robert North
19.DV8 Dance Company	Never Again, which deals with issues of homosexuality in society
20.Four by Kylian, an anthology	Svadebka
of modern ballets	La Cathédrale Engloutie
	Sinfonietta
	Torso
21.Riverdance	Various dance styles
22.That's Dancing	Various dances on film throughout this century

See Appendix (page 85) for details of video resources.

Glossary

Action and reaction – one or two movements which initiate a response of similar length

Aesthetic – concerned with appreciation through using the senses with imagination

Canon – two or more phrases of movement which recur or repeat, performed after an interval of time

Choreography – a finished dance work; the act of making dances

Composition – arrangement of parts to make a whole; a term applied across the art forms

Copy – movement which is exactly the same as another dancer

Dance style – the selection and use of the various constituents of dance which combine to determine style

Dance technique – particular movement skills related to a certain form or style of dance

Do-si-do – back to back

Duet/duo – a dance for two people

Dynamics – the expressive quality and energy of movement which considers time, weight, space and flow

Focus – use of the eyes to enhance performance qualities, often referring to the dancer's line of sight

Form – overall shape and structure of the dance composition

Gallop – a leap in uneven rhythm

Gesture – a movement by a particular body part – e.g. head, shoulder, leg – that is non-weight bearing when moved

Improvisation – exploring and developing movement ideas imaginatively in response to a stimulus or task

Mirror – movement performed as in a mirror image

Motif – a simple phrase of movement that contains within it something that is capable of being developed

Phrase – a sequence of dance movement that has a shape in time and has an ending

Plié – a knee bend

Polka – step, step, step, hop

Promenade – a two-hand hold with a partner

Question and answer – a short phrase of movement which initiates another phrase of movement in response

Sequence, a – one movement followed by another creates a sequence

Set sequence/set dance study – a precise series of movements which should be performed exactly as taught, emphasising technical skill and expressive qualities

Skip, a – a step hop in uneven rhythm

Syncopation – accenting a normally unaccented beat, or the absence of an accent where one is expected

Tendu – stretched (often used to describe a stretched foot)

Technique – movement skill

Transition – the link between movements, phrases or sections of a dance

Trio – a dance for three people

Type of dance – a broad classification of dances which includes e.g. abstract, comic, dance-drama, dramatic, lyrical, a study

Unison – movement performed at the same time as another dancer within the group

1 Introduction

Let's Look at Dance! is about:

- Teaching dance in the National Curriculum at Key Stages 1, 2 and 3, at GCSE and 'A' level, and on further and higher education courses through the use of professional dance on video as a resource.
- Helping dance teachers whether non-specialist or specialist access information to help raise the quality and effectiveness of teaching and learning in dance.
- Developing young people's ability to learn from looking at dance, using the visual medium as a learning style.

It provides teachers with:

- Knowledge of what video resources are available and how to purchase them.
- Guidance on how to use the video as a teaching approach.
- Suggestions on methodology to develop the range of teaching and learning strategies.
- Ideas for dance content to enable them to plan units and schemes of work.
- Detailed examples of dance frameworks and suggestions for musical accompaniment.
- A range of dance styles which will help to extend their own and children's dance experience.
- Material that could be used as distance learning resources on professional development courses.
- Support and guidance to develop their expertise and confidence in teaching dance.

The material in this book has been generated through several years of research with children, students and teachers in a variety of teaching and learning contexts. Our approach to the use of professional dance on video as a teaching and learning methodology has been developed through exploring the potential of video as a resource, analysing, reviewing and refining our work.

There is an ever-increasing range of dance material available on video which can be purchased commercially. It is also worth noting that recording dance from the television, whether it is a dance feature or an extract from a film or arts programme, can considerably supplement resources.

Types of video recordings include the following. All of those referred to are included in the text:

- Classical ballet performed by large dance companies, e.g. *Still Life at the Penguin Café* and *The Tales of Beatrix Potter* by the Royal Ballet.
- Performance and discussion of specific dance styles within a cultural context, e.g. *Gift of Tradition,* showing South Asian dance, and *The Path,* showing Afro-Caribbean dance.

- Contemporary dance featuring the work of modern choreographers, e.g. *Troy Game* by Robert North and *Ghost Dances* by Christopher Bruce.
- Modern dance works which have a strong narrative and dramatic content, e.g. *L'Enfant et les Sortilèges* by Jiri Kylian and *Late Flowering Lust* by Matthew Bourne.
- Musicals which feature dance performed in a variety of styles, e.g. *Singin' in the Rain* by Gene Kelly and *West Side Story* by Jerome Robbins (Figure 1.1).
- Dances designed to be used intentionally as a teaching resource. These are often accompanied by notes and resource packs, e.g. *Where Angels Fear to Tread* by V.TOL.
- Contemporary dance performed by a small-scale professional group, e.g. *Anarkos* by Random Dance Company.
- Dance analysis, which looks at specific features of the work, e.g. *Rushes* by Siobhan Davies (not discussed in this text).

Owing to the growing number of professional dance works now available on video, it has been necessary to make a selection from these to include in the book. We have based our video choices upon:

- Suitability of dance content for teaching and learning.
- Availability at time of publication.
- Purchase cost – unfortunately some video resources were deemed too expensive for general use in education.

Selecting an appropriate dance on video can be a lengthy and time-consuming process. One of the aims of this book is to provide information on the range of dance material available on video, so that teachers can select their resources more easily. We have made reference to videos which collectively include various dance styles, the work of different choreographers and reflect the dance of several cultures. Teachers will need to consider which dance will best suit their requirements.

Figure 1.1 West Side Story.© Bill Cooper

2   Using Professional Dance on Video as a Teaching and Learning Resource

The Importance of Learning through Looking at Dance

Dance often uses movement symbolically to create meaning and communicate ideas and feelings. Owing to its abstract nature the meaning is not pre-determined or designated but open to a wide range of individual interpretation. Dance education introduces children to this particular symbolic mode of thinking, doing and feeling through providing them with opportunities to *create, perform* and *view* dance. These three interrelated strands underpin the teaching and learning of dance, and the use of professional dance on video can enrich and extend children's skills, knowledge and understanding.

The viewing of dance should be devised to inform children's understanding through attending to objective features in the work. Whilst the analysis may consist of pulling the dance apart to investigate particular elements it should also be used to identify general principles which guide and support the art of choreography. However, this must be combined with opportunities for children to respond intuitively to what they see and feel through exercising their imagination:

- It may be necessary to watch the piece several times so that, with guidance from the teacher, children can develop the skills to describe, explain, interpret and evaluate the work.
- As their knowledge of dance increases children should be encouraged to go beyond merely expressing personal preferences to justify and support their opinions with reference to objective features of the dance.
- An essential aspect of this process is also the development of an aesthetic response to the piece; what feelings does it evoke? What sensations does it stimulate? How does it affect you? Through articulating their feelings about the dance a contribution is made to children's aesthetic education.

The interrelationship between intellectual analysis and imaginative, intuitive engagement with the dance is an essential aspect of developing children's dance appreciation. Acknowledging that this is a complex process, less experienced children will initially observe and describe the dance before developing the intellectual ability to analyse the work with knowledge and understanding of dance conventions and traditions.

Professional dance on video as a resource for teaching and learning

The elements of professional dance that need to be considered when planning tasks to support the teaching and learning of dance are shown below.

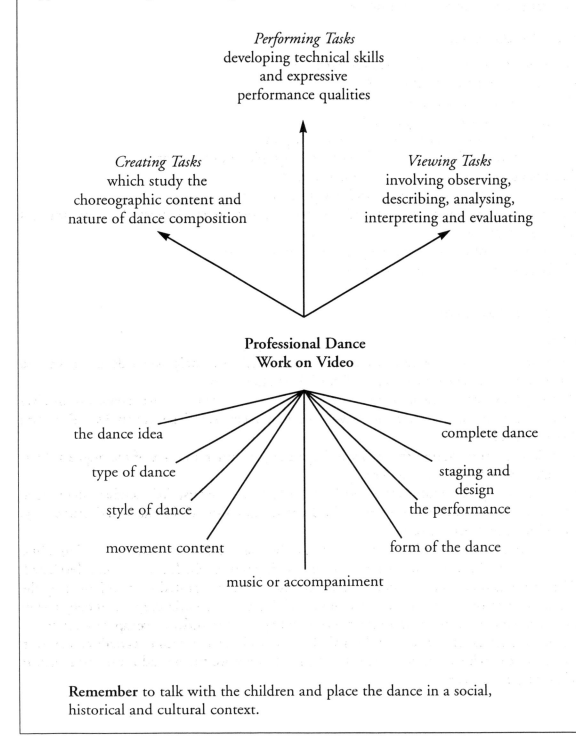

Performing Tasks
developing technical skills
and expressive
performance qualities

Creating Tasks
which study the
choreographic content and
nature of dance composition

Viewing Tasks
involving observing,
describing, analysing,
interpreting and evaluating

**Professional Dance
Work on Video**

the dance idea

type of dance

style of dance

movement content

music or accompaniment

complete dance

staging and
design

the performance

form of the dance

Remember to talk with the children and place the dance in a social, historical and cultural context.

How to plan for the use of professional dance on video

It is essential to determine the purposes of showing children the video and identify learning outcomes related to creating, performing and viewing dance.

Guiding questions for the teacher

Is the video chosen to:

- Stimulate work on a similar theme/idea/mood?
- Illustrate a specific style of dance?
- Provide ideas for movement content?
- Suggest ways of composing dance?
- Demonstrate a particular aspect of dance composition?
- Exemplify the work of a certain dancer, choreographer or company?
- Place dance in an historical or cultural context?
- Illustrate the use of costume, set and design in dance?
- Develop musical understanding and demonstrate the range of musical accompaniment selected for dance works?
- Improve skills of description, analysis and interpretation?
- Challenge preconceptions about dance?

Setting Children tasks

Creating

- Using the video to provide ideas as a stimulus which may help when deciding what to dance about, and extend the range of possible starting points.
- Showing how the dance idea can be translated into movement; this frequently involves transforming the literal actions into symbolic movement, e.g. 'The Tennis Dance' in *Late Flowering Lust*.
- Stimulating improvisation through viewing a range of different ways of moving, e.g. 'The Cat Dance' in *L'Enfant et Les Sortilèges*.
- Demonstrating the significance of relationships between dancers, their gender and number, and how they are used in the space can be discussed to inform children's own decisions, e.g. The Ghosts in *Ghost Dances*.
- Setting compositional tasks which are exemplified in a dance extract, e.g. in *Troy Game* watch the duet in which the two men use a hopping action which is varied and developed. Discuss the action content and how the movement idea is repeated with variations by the 2 dancers. Use the duet as a starting point for children's own work; they might copy one or two of the movements or create their own hopping ideas in order to compose a motif.
- Giving examples of the use of formal devices, such as repetition, variation, contrast, transition etc. which can be observed and used to improve the overall form and structure of dances, e.g. *Anarkos*.

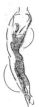

● Exemplifying the characteristic features of choreography (i) by certain choreographers, e.g. Christopher Bruce who combines ballet, folk and contemporary dance to create an original movement language, (ii) in certain dance styles e.g. African where floor patterns and group shapes are used to create visual interest.

Performing

● Copying two or three movements from the professional dance which will enrich the children's movement vocabulary and also develop their skills of observation. These could be adapted and modified if necessary whilst still extending their repertoire of movement, e.g. 'Jeremy Fisher's Dance' in *The Tales of Beatrix Potter* (Figure 2.1).

● Identifying the characteristic features of a particular dance style, and practising the technical skills which underpin it, such as the isolated movement patterns of jazz dance, which can then improve performance, e.g. *West Side Story* (Figure 2.2).

Figure 2.1 The Tales of Beatrix Potter. © Bill Cooper

● Learning a set study or sequence based upon the professional dance which requires technical accuracy as well as expressive performance. This will frequently concentrate on a limited range of movement material that will present a challenge for the children to master, e.g. 'Mrs TiggyWinkle's Washing Dance' in *The Tales of Beatrix Potter*, or a South Asian Dance from a *Gift of Tradition*.

Figure 2.2 West Side Story. © Bill Cooper

● Copying body shapes from photographs or the video, e.g. 'Kangaroo Rat Dance' in *Still Life at the Penguin Café* (Figure 2.3).

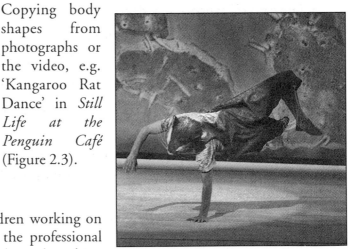

Figure 2.3 Still Life at the Penguin Café. © Bill Cooper

Viewing

Viewing is often the forerunner to children working on creating or performing tasks related to the professional dance work and needs to be part of the planned teaching approach.

Children will need to be provided with guidance to inform and structure their looking as it is not an easy task to watch dance perceptively due to its transitory nature. It cannot be contemplated over time in the same way that a painting or sculpture may be.

Figure 2.4. Late Flowering Lust. © Bill Cooper

The video resource will enable them to watch professional dance, perhaps for the first time, and be given opportunities to respond to the work. Through the use of the video they can revisit the dance, providing time for reflection and the acquisition of new skills and knowledge.

Children may be provided with:

● Opportunities for discussion, involving prepared questions to focus on certain features of the dance, which encourages the use of a growing vocabulary to express thoughts and convey meaning.

● Written worksheets to complete which develop their skills, knowledge and understanding of dance.

● Information which places the dance in a social, cultural or historical context. For example *Late Flowering Lust* (Figure 2.4) illustrates the lifestyle of a particular class of society in the 1930s; it features the poetry of John Betjeman who is commenting on his own life and it is also representative of the work of Matthew Bourne, a contemporary choreographer.

Looking at professional dance will involve the children in observing, describing, analysing, interpreting and evaluating the work. Elements will include:

● The original dance idea, e.g. was it an imaginative starting point?

● The type of dance, e.g. a dance-drama, an abstract dance.

● The dance style, e.g. ballet, South Asian or folk.

● The movement content, e.g. was it relevant and varied or clichéd?

● The music or accompaniment, e.g. was it appropriate?

● The form of the dance, e.g. use of motifs, variation and development of movement, repetition.

● The performance, e.g. was it danced with technical skill and expression?

● The staging and design, e.g. were the costumes suitable, did the stage/set enhance the dance idea?

● The complete dance, e.g. was it interesting and worth watching?

How to teach through the use of professional dance on video

Integral to the planning process will be questions about how to teach using the video material. Having made decisions about the choice of video resource consideration needs to be given to the teaching strategies that will be most beneficial to children's learning. There

are a number of options available and the specific teaching context will necessarily influence the decisions teachers make. Should it be shown at the start of a lesson, during practical work, or at the end of a lesson? These decisions will be part of planning and may well be reconsidered as the work progresses.

The video material should be used flexibly, with the teacher exerting professional judgement about precisely how and when it will be employed.

The following strategies have evolved through working with teachers and children, and are practical suggestions for incorporating the video material into a lesson, unit of work or scheme of work. Through using observation, discussion, description, analysis and interpretation of the specific dance children's understanding can be developed.

1. Show a short extract (2-3 minutes) before starting any practical work

Show it several times. This could be used to illustrate a style of dance through observation and identification of the characteristic movement features. Children could then be encouraged to include these in their own work, having seen an example of a professional performance. The aim is not to replicate the dance performance but to develop an awareness of the movement style which can inform their own choreography, performance and viewing of dance.

Looking at a piece of South Asian or jazz dance can given an immediate visual impression of how that style can be represented rather than trying to describe it aurally. The visual impact can be strengthened with each showing by directing children's attention to specific features, for example the use of stylised hand and arm gestures in South Asian dance, thereby increasing their dance knowledge. References to the video can then enhance the teaching through making use of the children's direct experience, which the whole class has been engaged in, during subsequent practical work.

It may be beneficial to watch the extract three or four times at the outset and then view it again as the work progresses.

2. Show a section or piece of a dance work which might stimulate work on a similar theme or topic before starting the practical work

This could be used to generate ideas and discussion about how movement can be used to tell a story or express a mood. For example:

- The Tennis Dance in *Late Flowering Lust* could be used to show how literal movement can be made more dance like. This knowledge could then be applied to other sporting dance ideas such as swimming or the Olympic Games.

- The three ghosts in *Ghost Dances* who create a strange and eerie mood (Figure 2.5) could be used to exemplify other unworldly characters and a narrative might unfold.

3. Use the whole dance work

This might be shown in smaller sections in order to study it as one might a written text or piece of music from the repertoire. The movement content, style and overall form could be evaluated and used to inform children's understanding of dance.

Figure 2.5 Ghost Dances. © Jack Mitchell

4. Start working on a dance idea

Then show a piece of video that demonstrates the movement qualities, choreographic ideas, group relationships etc. that you are working on with the children. This can then be used as impetus for their own work.

5. Having taught a dance study show the video extract upon which it is based

Identify the similarities and recognise the differences between the two pieces.

6. Watch a short extract that demonstrates an aspect of choreography

For example motif development or the use of repetition. Discuss how it affects the work and relate it to their own dance composition. Practical tasks could then be set which include the use of these devices.

7. Watch several extracts from the work of a particular dancer, choreographer or company

Make comparisons and identify the stylistic features. This analysis could provide the basis for a composition reflecting this style or a reconstruction of a recognised dance work.

8. As part of their cultural education show video extracts which reflect different traditions and influences

Examples include African and Caribbean dance. These could be used to develop and enrich their understanding of the lifestyle of people in other countries and the significance of dance in that culture.

How children learn through the use of professional dance on video

Learning can take place in many different ways and some will suit certain children better than others. They may be able to select the strategies which best meet their needs. The dance on video may be used to:

- Provide movement content which the children can *copy* or *imitate.*

- Set practical *problem-solving tasks,* with some examples being shown in the professional dance, e.g. different ways of hopping or jumping.

- Promote *discussion and develop a language* to talk about dance through describing, interpreting and evaluating the work.

- Encourage children to *write about* or *draw what they see* in the dance.

- Provide examples of excellence in dance performance and composition, which can motivate them to *practise,* make progress and strive for quality in their own work through a *disciplined* approach to study.

- Improve their *observational* skills and ability to *concentrate.*

- Encourage new and original responses through developing children's *imagination* in dance.

- Learn more about their feelings and emotions through the opportunity to *watch* dance and respond to it.

- Promote *independent* and *collaborative* work demonstrating the capacity for *sustained study* and good *interpersonal skills.*
  (See the *OFSTED Handbook.*)

3 Guidance on Using the Selected Professional Dance Works

Using the selected professional dance work

The following details are provided for each dance recording:

1. The synopsis.
2. Dance ideas.
3. Discussion and video analysis
4. Evaluation and appreciation.
5. Dance framework and choreographic tasks.
6. Music.
7. Photographs.

1. The Synopsis

The synopsis of the dance work which provides background information and places it in a context, whether historical, cultural or social, to assist with the video analysis and discussion.

2. Dance Ideas

These suggest starting points for dance taken from the video.

3. Discussion and Video Analysis

Guidance is given to help teachers develop children's critical and analytical skills when looking at the dance. The questions are designed to focus attention on three main aspects:

1. *Movement content* – The use of:
   a) Action – what is the movement, e.g. travel, jump?
   b) Space – where is the movement happening, e.g. forwards, high or low?
   c) Dynamics – how is the movement being performed, e.g. fast, strong?
2. *Composition* – The use of:
   a) Choreographic devices, e.g. unison, canon, mirroring.
   b) Elements which provide compositional form, e.g. repetition, contrast, highlights.
3. *Overall style and expression* – The word style can be used in several different ways. In this

text it usually applies to the type or kind of dance, which is determined by all its constituent features, e.g. South Asian dance, jazz dance. The dance needs to be placed in a context and this could include comparisons with work in a similar or contrasting style.

Other important elements of the dance may also need to be discussed, such as:

● Musical accompaniment, e.g. the tempo, timbre, instruments used, musical style.
● Costume, e.g. does it suggest a character? Is it designed to enhance the movement?
● Set design and lighting, e.g. does it create a mood or atmosphere? Does it suggest a time or place?

4. Evaluation and Appreciation

The children should be encouraged to reflect on their aesthetic perceptions of the dance alongside an analysis of the work. For example:

● What did it make them think of?
● How did they feel when watching it?
● What was significant to them, did parts of the dance stand out and if so why?
● What meaning did they detect, what did they imagine the dance was about?

(See Appendix, page 87/8.)

5. Dance Frameworks and Choreographic Tasks

We have chosen to present the material for dancers depending upon their prior experience of dance. Some ideas will be more appropriate for younger or older children. However, the content will frequently depend not upon their chronological age but the children's previous level of attainment in dance.

Dance frameworks are designed to suggest an outline structure or skeleton of the dance. They provide the scaffolding around which the children create movement content and develop their own ideas. The frameworks can be altered and adapted to suit:

● the age and experience of the dancers
● the length of time available
● the expertise of the teacher.

They are only intended as a guide and should not be considered in any way prescriptive, nor do they need to follow the suggested order:

1. *Simple dance frameworks* – These are relatively short and easy frameworks for less experienced dancers.

2. *More experienced dancers* – These frameworks are more complex and could be used to challenge more experienced dancers of various ages.

3. *Dance framework ideas* – These are designed to help students and teachers structure their own dances. They are suggestions which may be combined with other ideas to choreograph a complete dance.

When planning a framework it is worth considering some of the following questions:

- What style of music is most appropriate – does this provide a structure for the dance; e.g. are there repetitions, chorus and verse sections?
- Is there a variety of movement content in the dance, e.g. a range of actions, contrasting dynamics, use of levels and different directions?
- Is the dance a solo, a duet, a small/large group or whole class piece, or does it include several of these group relationships?
- Are there any choreographic devices included, e.g. unison, canon, question and answer, to guide the compositional process?
- How does the dance start and finish?
- Is there an overall sense of form, e.g. beginning, middle and end?
- Does the composition include repetition, development, contrast and highlights?
- Does the dance develop logically?
- Are there fluent transitions between the sections?
- Do the children have opportunities to answer a variety of closed and open-ended tasks?

A dance framework will usually have:

- A clear beginning, middle and end.
- Phrases of movement which are repeated.
- Some elements of contrast in action, dynamics, space or use of group relationships.
- Some type of auditory accompaniment to which it is performed.

In this sense it begins to resemble the form of a complete dance. Sometimes this may be very simple and for the sake of involving the whole class may include sections which are repeated by different small groups. As the children will frequently create much of the movement content they will decide on the selection and refinement of that movement and how to pattern it into a phrase. The teacher acts as an informed guide, observing, discussing and sharing ideas with the children as they work. The whole class may participate in shaping the final piece, including how it starts and ends, what is the best use of available space, does it require a sense of 'front' to perform to, should different dancers or groups take on particular roles in the dance? Providing opportunities for children to watch each other's work will help them with these decisions and can also improve the quality of their own work. This may be done through watching a partner dance, 2 children watching another 2, a small group observing another group's work or half the class watching the other half. The more provision that is made for children to look at dance the greater the possibilities are for increasing their awareness and knowledge of dance. With a focus for their viewing children can begin to evaluate each other's work and through reciprocal teaching develop their own and their peers' skills.

6. Music

Ideas are given for music to accompany each dance. In several cases the original music is available and details are given in the list of audio resources in the Appendix.

7. Photographs

These may be used as an additional visual resource and include photographs of professional dancers as well as children dancing (Figures 3.1 and 3.2). Each photograph illustrates a particular aspect of the dance on video.

Figure 3.1 Child dancing Singin' in the Rain.
© Bill Cooper.

Figure 3.2 Children dancing Troy Game. © Bill Cooper.

4 Details of the Professional Dance Videos and Dance Frameworks

VIDEO TITLE	## An Evening with Rambert Dance Company. Sergeant Early's Dream

Choreographed by Christopher Bruce.

Premier in 1984 by Ballet Rambert at the Marlowe Theatre, Canterbury.

Synopsis

The theme of the ballet is a universal one: the sadness of being uprooted. Bruce draws on historical information about the immigration to the New World (America) at the time of the mid-nineteenth century potato famines in Ireland; however, the work could relate to any displaced people.

Bruce has written a programme note:

> There is a theme woven into the piece connected with the migration from the old world to the new. Throughout there is a feeling of sadness at leaving the old home and losing touch with old roots. However, people take with them threads of their own culture which will inevitably develop separately.

Bruce has created a sequence of 10 distinct dances to Anglo-Irish and American folk music, some of it instrumental, some vocal. Although the music is folk the choreography extends and develops the traditional movement content. Speaking in an interview prior to the work's American premier Bruce said:

> 'I was trying to create a collage of ideas so I used a base of folk dance. But I've invented my own steps.... You go back to a very simple truth, and those truths will supply you with very simple movements. And from that you can build.'

The dancers wear simple costumes reflecting the folk influence, with the women in long skirts whose swirling movement enhances the visual impact of the lyrical choreography.

The ensemble of seven musicians are dressed similarly to the dancers and perform on stage, playing uileann pipes, whistles, fiddles, guitars and drums like a folk band. The music fluctuates in mood, from need and despair to joy and flirtation, including light-hearted and comical ideas. Folk songs provide the inspiration for the individual dances and without building a narrative suggest the bitter-sweet mixture of hope and sadness connected with the theme of migration from old world to new.

Dance Content (running order as on the video)

Section 1: May Morning Dew/Sergeant Early's Dream (Full company)

The words of the first song tell of an emigrant who returns home from abroad to find that everything he once knew has changed. The dance suggests a longing for a past left behind, creating a wistful quality as the company slowly and supportively dance with each other.

The sad mood is broken when the non-vocal tune, *Sergeant Early's Dream*, is played and one lone dancer recalls a variety of folk dances. The movement is influenced by the hornpipe and Irish step dancing, and both the men and women join in this lively and joyful piece.

Section 2: Eighteen Years Old (Duet for two women)

This song tells the story of a mother and daughter who are discussing marriage. The movement content frequently uses images in the lyrics to create motifs and there are many circular gestures, body shapes and floor patterns.

Section 3: The Kylebrack Rambler/Shipsave Sailing/Richard Dwyer's (Full company)

Three reels which are fast and rhythmic provide the inspiration for a slapstick fight, a flirtatious dance and a dance for the four men. Elements of folk dancing are evident throughout this section.

Section 4: Geordie (Duet for a man and a woman)

This ballad tells the story of a man who is to be hung for stealing and selling the king's deer. The female dancer is his wife who is mourning her husband's fate and the male dancer overhears her story and provides some support. Again there are explicit references to the lyrics in the symbolic movement motifs.

Section 5: Love Will You Marry Me/Plains of Boyle (One woman and four men)

This song and instrumental accompanies a humorous dance in which the woman flirts with the men but ends up alone.

Section 6: Black is the Colour of My True Love's Hair (Duet for a man and a woman)

An evocative and intense love song based on traditional lyrics which are reflected in the couple's relationship and fluctuating moods.

Section 7: Peggy Gordon (Three men and one woman)

A comical dance for three 'drunken' men, observed by a disapproving woman, which uses movement based on falling, catching and supporting as well as steps from previous sections.

Section 8: Gospel Ship (Solo for a woman)

This gospel song accompanies a lively and carefree dance which includes many folk dance elements and stylised tap-dance steps.

Section 9: Barbara Allen (Four men and four women)

The dancers use literal gestures to express the story in this ballad.

Section 10: Junior Crehan's Favourite/Corney is Coming/Se Fadh Mo Bhuadhra (Full company)

This series of three instrumental tunes starts quietly but gradually develops into a lively and rhythmic piece. The dancers perform a folk dance which echoes and repeats movement content from earlier sections. It concludes in a reflective and wistful mood, recalling the opening of the dance.

Dance Ideas

1. There are elements of folk dance in many of the sections, including Irish step dancing and jigs, a barndance, a hornpipe, heel and toe steps and flexed feet. These could provide a range of steps and step patterns which would form the basic movement content for a dance evocative of folk dancing. (Sections 1, 3, 8 and 10 in particular.)

Figure 4.1 Sergeant Early's Dream. © Bill Cooper.

2. The three duets (Sections 2, 4 and 6) could be used as examples of narrative where the choreography of movement motifs is based mainly upon the song lyrics. These literal images are abstracted and developed throughout each duet.

3. The comical nature of Sections 3, 5 and 7 might inspire a humorous work where the playful interaction between the dancers is expressively significant.

4. The overall theme of the work could provide a starting point for a choreography connected with ideas of migration, a sense of loss and nostalgia in changing times which also captures the folk culture and power of folk music (*see Framework*).

Discussion and Video Analysis – A Dramatic Folk Dance

Watch Sections 1 and 10 and focus on:

- the mood and expressive qualities in the dance,
- the movement content,
- the folk dance style.

Section 1(a) May Morning Dew

1. Identify the **action content** which suggests a yearning for the past, mutual support and care for each other such as
   (a) walking in two's, sometimes in contact,
   (b) the use of reaching gestures,
   (c) gently lifting and lowering one another,
   (d) supporting each other.

2. Discuss how the **movement qualities** convey the mood, e.g. sustained, smooth, fluent actions.

Section 1(b) Sergeant Early's Dream

3. Select the steps and gestures which reflect the lively, rhythmic influence of the **hornpipe,** e.g. arms folded across the body, elbows lifted, rocking movements from side to side, heel and toe steps, and **Irish step dancing,** e.g. upright posture, arms by the side, high knee lift, stepping on the spot with precise footwork.

Section 10 Finale

4. Identify the movement content from Section 1 which is repeated to create a joyous 'ceilidh'. Notice how the atmosphere changes as the dance ends, returning to the sad and reflective mood portrayed at the beginning of the dance.

A Dramatic Folk Dance – A Simple Framework

Stimulus

Take a simple storyline of:

1. People emigrating from their homeland and wishing that they could return.

2. Remembering the good times.

3. Finally accepting their new life.

			Teaching points
Section 1	A	Individually or in twos choose a starting position which shows sadness and longing.	Use different levels and directions
		Slowly start to move using walks, include moments of stillness. Develop through adding arm gestures reaching out into space, to a partner, to other members of the group and create a simple motif.	Emphasise the use of focus. The arm gestures could use 1 or 2 arms, encourage the use of diagonals.
	B	Travel in contact with a partner, e.g. (1) hold hands or link arms, (2) arm around or on partner's shoulder. Repeat and/ or develop the reaching motif as a duet. The development could include (1) lowering and lifting your partner from the floor, (2) supporting and leaning movements.	Stress sensitivity to your partner.
Section 2	C	Individually create a short motif using hornpipe and Irish steps and gestures. Perform as (1) a solo, and/or (2) a duet being aware of a partner, and/or (3) a duet using question and answer, unison.	Encourage repetition of simple steps and clear arm positions.
	D	Create a duet using question and answer, and unison including movements from the solo motifs.	This task would be more appropriate for dancers with some experience.
	E	Whole group dance using traditional folkdance patterns and figures to create a lively ending.	Use simple steps such as skips, walks and gallops.
Section 3	F	Repeat and develop elements of Section 1 to conclude the dance and decide on the final mood.	

More experienced dancers could learn selected movement content from the video in each section. The piece could be choreographed as a small group dance for 6–8 dancers exploring the potential of working in two's, three's, four's, etc.

Learning Outcomes

Children should be guided to:

- *Composing* – Explore and select movement content which expresses ideas, feelings/moods and create simple phrases.
- *Performing* – Perform actions with different qualities of speed, tension and continuity to show changes in expression. Dance with an awareness of a partner and the group so that the relationships are clear.
- *Appreciating* – Describe the movement content and narrative of the dance and interpret the feelings/meanings it conveys.

Music for the Dance

- The original music is available on CD (see Audio Resources Appendix, page 85).
- Traditional British/American folk songs and tunes, e.g. *Planxty, The Chieftans, Shannon Shannon, DeDannon, Capercaillie*
- The children could learn a folk song which could be recorded to accompany the dance. The lyrics would provide the narrative.

Figure 4.2 Sergeant Early's Dream: a dramatic folk dance. © Bill Cooper.

| VIDEO TITLE | # An Evening with Rambert Dance Company. Lonely Town, Lonely Street |

Choreographed by Robert North.

Premier in 1980 by the Janet Smith Dance Group at Phoenix Arts Centre, Leicester. First performed by Ballet Rambert at Grand Theatre, Leeds, 1981.

Synopsis

Set to a series of seven Bill Wither's songs, this ballet uses the jazz dance style to convey a lonely and desolate scene. The stage design reflects life in a downtown inner city area, with illuminated signs, a fire escape and overflowing rubbish bins. The company of four women and three men wear contemporary clothes of the 1980s, including bomber jackets and jeans, lending an authentic 'streetfeel' to the work. The lyrics in each song provide the dramatic themes, including isolation, rejection, self-pity and confrontation.

Dance Content (running order as on the video)

Section 1

The company use simple walks and runs to create floor patterns which are continuously changing direction and weaving in and out, whilst avoiding eye contact with each other. This creates a busy, confused feeling where each individual is isolated even though part of a crowd. When dancers try to make contact with each other they are ignored and rejected.

Section 2

A male dancer awakes from a nightmare and performs a lurching, falling solo suggesting he is on the run or may be under the influence of drinks or drugs. He is beset by three women who appear to be predatory and hostile.

Section 3

A duet between a man and a woman which has a fluid, lyrical quality, reflecting her longing for a former love and the man's desire to become a part of her life. They almost come together but sadly she leaves him on his own.

Section 4

'I don't want you on my mind' are the repetitive, driving lyrics of this song and the dance starts and finishes with the three men defiantly dancing without the women.

Section 5

A duet between Robert North (the choreographer) and Lucy Burge provides dramatic tension in the story. Jealous of her attention to another man he manipulates her physically, using lifts, supports, and throws as the lyrics ask 'Who is he and what is he to you?'. The movement quickens in pace until it is resolved when the woman leaves.

Section 6

A male solo of self-pitying desolation follows this rejection, demonstrating the fluent but precise qualities of this dance style.

Section 7

The finalé involves the whole company in an up-tempo dance with constantly changing groupings. Filmed through parts of the set with the camera out of the horizontal alignment, the whole piece has a sense of off-balanced frenzy. The movement uses head clasping gestures and sudden jerky actions.

Dance Ideas

1. A city street dance focusing on ideas of rejection and isolation from the group, and exploring the feelings this evokes (*see Framework*).
2. A solo which depicts one or several of the moods conveyed in the dance, such as loneliness, rejection, sadness or instability.
3. A set jazz study using the style of movement shown on the video.

Jazz Dance Style in this dance

The elements which demonstrate jazz dance influences are:

- Action content such as jumps and turns, which are part of the typical, stylised movement vocabulary of jazz dance.
- Action content which uses isolated body parts, e.g. head and arm gestures.
- Contractions of the torso.
- The lack of turnout but use of parallel position and inversion.
- Sudden changes of dynamics and spatial patterns.
- Changing rhythm patterns and the use of syncopation.

Lonely Town, Lonely Street reflects a particular style of jazz dance which includes fluent and lyrical qualities not always associated with this technique. North has dedicated the work to Matt Mattox, who originally created this style.

Discussion and Video Analysis – A City Street Dance

Watch Section 1, focus on how the unfriendly 'streetfeel' mood is conveyed through the changing group relationships and use of gestures to reject and isolate individuals.

Stimulus

Take the idea of the outsider(s) in society and peer group exclusion: how does it feel to be the odd one out and not accepted? Aspects of bullying could also be explored. Pictures might provide additional ideas, where body shapes suggest dominance, rejection or support.

A City Street Dance – The Outsider, a Simple Framework

A small group or whole class dance	Teaching points
A Create an individual walking pattern, include changes of direction and rhythm. Repeat several times. Introduce a set walking pattern to the whole class. This could be taken from the video or drawn from the student's own work. Gradually increase the number of dancers performing the step in unison. Retain a sense of wariness as separate individuals within the group	Encourage clear floor patterns and the use of focus to express isolation.
B In a trio explore the idea of rejection using ideas such as: 1. turning away 2. shrugging somebody off 3. staring someone out 4. pushing against others Include 3/4 still group shapes to provide contrast	Include body contact, this may need guidance such as stressing the use of different body parts to push, pull or support each other.
C Developments could include (1) trio split up and repeat walking patterns in 'A' to create a whole class ending; (2) trio develop a sense of unity and walk together to meet up with another 3 to create a gang conflict scenario. Using action and reaction include jumps, turns and kicks to suggest a non-contact fight. Use words such as 'over', 'under' and 'around' to add variety to the spatial patterns. Resolve ending to convey group feeling; this might suggest harmony or discord, acceptance or rejection.	(2) The non-contact fight needs to be performed with accuracy and clarity, stress the physical skills required such as control, co-ordination and balance. Exaggerating the movement content and creating rhythmic phrases will create a more dance-like effect. Include moments of stillness to add dramatic tension.

More experienced dancers could use the jazz dance style throughout the work, incorporating some of the elements identified in the movement content. A set study could also be included which developed their technical performing skills through teaching steps taken from the video. Comparisons could be made with the video of *West Side Story*, which also explores relationships using jazz dance and music.

Learning Outcomes

Children should be guided to:
- *Composing* – create action phrases whose dynamic and spatial features depict mood and feeling.
- *Performing* – control actions with contrasting dynamic qualities and show clarity in body shape and pathways.
- *Appreciating* – comment on the stimulus and the dance outcome, and offer their opinion.

Music for the Dance

- Recordings of Bill Withers songs as used on the video.
- Contemporary songs whose lyrics express similar moods and feelings, e.g. Eric Clapton.
- Instrumental jazz music which has a blues feel.

Dance Theatre of Harlem. Troy Game

Choreographed by Robert North.

Premier in 1974 in Liverpool by London Contemporary Dance Theatre (LCDT).
Performed on the video by Dance Theatre of Harlem.

Synopsis

Robert North introduces this dance on the video and explains how the original dance
idea evolved. The company had just returned from Brazil where they had seen Capoeira,
a stylised form of fighting and dancing set to the rhythms of Batucada, ethnic music from
Brazil. The influence of the martial arts, including Aikido and Tai Chi which they had also
studied, combined with the rhythmic music provided the stimulus for the choreography.
As North explains he wanted to create a piece that involves "dancing to music" and also
"making fun of macho men". He therefore displays the athletic musculature and prowess
of the male dancers whilst at the same time not allowing them to take themselves too
seriously:

> 'The title comes from a book by Lincoln Kirstein (founder of New York City Ballet) and harks back to
> the days when dance was still considered a masculine pursuit; hence the costumes, reminiscent of Spartan
> warriors (who used to dance before going forth into battle) or Roman gladiators, although the socks
> suggest modern football players and a contemporary theme.'
>
> Video notes by Debra Craine (1992), R M Arts

The strength and stamina of the male dancer is taken to the limit by North's choreography
and eventually the company collapse with exhaustion!

Dance Content (running order as on the video)

The dance falls into several sections of different lengths.

Section 1

Introduction and warming-up – this starts in silence with the six dancers performing strong,
powerful movements and holding clear body shapes, as the rhythmic music starts they
progress into a series of exercises.

Section 2

Martial arts – the light-hearted mood changes to concentrate and focus the viewer on a solo
dancer who performs sequences influenced by the martial arts. At first he gestures, kicks,
turns, and rolls to the accompaniment of a haunting, oriental score and is then joined by five
other dancers who echo his movement style mirroring and copying each other in twos.

Section 3

Ensemble piece – the lively rhythmic music returns to accompany the 12 male dancers who
perform 'Capoeira style' fighting moves in unison in a strong, up-tempo section.

Section 4

Virtuoso section – individual dancers display their physical prowess:

a. A solo dancer performs a dazzling series of jumps with spectacular body shapes.

b. A light-hearted duet based on hopping, or dancing on one leg, in which the 2 dancers try to out-do one another.

c. Two more solos based on leaping, turning and jumping with great technical skill.

Section 5

Solo dancer and the company – humorous section in which the soloist is prevented from leaving the stage by the other dancers. He eventually outwits them as they chase him to and fro across the space.

Section 6

Finalé – this includes the comic scene of one dancer who will not stop dancing, despite the efforts of the others, and builds up to a high-energy sequence of explosive leaps, jumps and runs, ending as the dancers collapse from exhaustion.

Dance Ideas

This work provides a variety of starting points and a selection taken from the following ideas could be incorporated into different dance frameworks suited to the age and experience of the children.

1. A solo virtuoso dance demonstrating technical skill (refer to Sections 4 and 6).

2. A light-hearted duet, one dancer trying to 'out-dance' their partner (refer to Sections 4b and 5, *see Framework*).

3. A duet based on the martial arts incorporating the elements of Tai Chi and Capoeira (refer to Sections 2 and 3, *see Framework*).

4. A duet or small group dance that includes the ideas of preparing for battle, demonstrating physical prowess and dancing until you drop, all performed in an athletic but light-hearted style (refer to Sections 1, 4b and 6, *see Framework*)

5. Group dance for 6–12 dancers using Sections 3 and 6 to create a choreography which is based purely on the movement content and style of the work. A variety of choreographic devices could be used to develop the piece. Children could devise their own motifs and be taught set studies from the video.

Discussion and Video Analysis

It would be appropriate to select the sections for analysis depending upon the dance framework.

Section 1

Start of the dance, dancers 'warming up':

1. *Identify a range of warm-up movement actions displaying strength and flexibility,* e.g. press-ups, hamstring stretch.

2. *Describe the movement qualities,* e.g. strong, powerful, athletic, direct, rhythmic.

3. *Comment on the different group relationships,* e.g. dancers working:
   (a) individually in a group
   (b) in unison
   (c) in trios with contrasting movements
   (d) as a group of six changing positions to hold shapes in contact.

Section 2

Martial Arts, starting with a solo dancer:

4. *Describe how the mood has changed,* e.g. music is quiet and haunting, movements are slower and more sustained.

5. *Identify the elements which indicate the influence of the martial arts,* e.g. stylised arm and hand gestures, strong use of focus, kicks and jumps, emphasis on control and precision of movement in space.

6. *As the six dancers perform in 2s identify the use of mirroring and copying.*

Section 4b

Hopping duet:

7. *Identify the main action in the duet,* i.e. hopping or dancing on one leg.

8. *Describe three variations of hopping,* e.g. (i) changing directions, (ii) leg lifted at the front and back, (iii) twisting upper body, (iv) boxing with the arms.

A Display of Physical Prowess – A Simple Framework

The start could be in silence as individuals hold clear poses as on the video.

A duet and group dance	Teaching points
A Choose 3 warm-up movements, repeat each in turn several times and link them together to make a phrase. Repeat the whole phrase 2 or 3 times (Section 1 on the video) 1. Perform individually or in 2s or 2. Develop the idea further in groups of 4–6 using unison/canon/question and answer or 3. Create a group motif using previous movement content or 4. In small groups devise a linear group shape, change positions in canon as on the video.	Stress clarity of body shape and action, fluent transitions and a sense of rhythm.
B In 2s perform a set motif using ideas from the video (Section 3) featuring rhythmic step patterns in unison, e.g.: 1. Walk a figure of eight, starting with the right foot taking 16 counts. 2. Perform a 'hopscotch step' on the spot x 4, i.e. jump 2 feet astride, hop on right, then jump 2 feet astride, hop on left. 3. Feet astride, knees bent, 8 small shuffles forward, right arm leading hand flexed upwards. 4. Jump feet together and crouch down, small backwards jump extending both arms up and leaning to the right. Repeat the whole movement leaning to the left, 4 times in total. Vary the motif through the use of canon, e.g. dancer A starts and dancer B moves after 8 counts.	Encourage accuracy of action content and awareness of the expressive qualities and spatial patterns. The style is strong and athletic.
C Select 3 different hopping ideas from the video (duet Section 4b) and create a short solo 'showing off' to a partner. Dancer A performs around partner, dancer B reacts on the spot, and vice versa.	Watch this short duet several times to allow the children to identify the variety of hopping steps which they might copy and adapt in their own 'virtuoso' solo.
D Using the 'boxing' ideas from the video (duet Section 4b) create an action and reaction sequence which travels to the sides of the space.	Whilst at the side encourage the dancers to keep moving before they re-enter for the final section.
E Ending – as in the final Section 6 of the video, one dancer re-enters the performing space and the others try to stop him moving, this could be staged with groups of 6 or 8 or the whole class. Decide on the finalé.	

Figure 4.3 Troy Game: a display of physical prowess. © Bill Cooper.

Learning Outcomes

Children should be guided to:

- *Composing* – Compose action phrases, motifs and sections of the dance and with guidance plan the whole dance.
- *Performing:*
  – Show clarity in body shape and action.
  – Demonstrate rhythm and musicality in their movement.
- *Appreciating* – Comment on the stimuli and how the powerful movement style on the video is reflected in their dance.

Music for the Dance

- Samba batucada has certain basic patterns and instrumentation that are common to each style. Hence samba played in Salvador de Bahia, though quite distinct from samba played in Rio, retains the two in a bar heavy back beat and the basic line up of bass drums, tamborines, snare, shaker and high-pitched solo drum or repinique.
- Inner Sense percussion tapes provide a range of rhythmic instrumentals including Batucada and Samba (see Audio Resources Appendix, page 85).
- Lively Brazilian instrumental music, e.g. Timbalada, Batucada (see Audio Resources Appendix, page 85).

Figure 4.4 Martial arts. © Bill Cooper.

Martial Arts – Simple Dance Framework

A duet (refer to Sections 2 and 3 in the video)	Teaching points
A Create a ritualistic greeting which is performed to a partner	Refer to the customs and traditions associated with the martial arts, also the Eastern influence.
B Teach a set step pattern based on the shape of a cross, i.e. standing with feet together, lunge to the right and return to centre, lunge to the left and return to centre, lunge forwards and return to centre, lunge backwards and return to centre moving only 1 foot at a time. Dancers select stylised arm gestures to accompany the step pattern to create a motif which they perform mirroring each other.	Encourage control and clarity of body shape, use both direct and flexible arm gestures, stress the need for focus and concentration to create a reflective mood. Include changes of speed to try to develop an awareness of the rhythm of the motif.
C Develop the motif in B through adding a jump, turn or kick and repeat, still mirroring.	Use ideas from the video to increase the range of movement vocabulary. Adapt and copy some of the duet work.
D Create a non-contact fight sequence, use the words over, under and around to shape the movement. Include one of the movements using physical contact from the video.	
E Ending – this could include a repetition of B and finish with A.	

Learning Outcomes

Children should be guided to:
- *Composing:*
  – Compose a motif and develop it through adding action content and varying the dynamics.
  – Use mirroring with a partner.
- *Performing* – demonstrate clear body shapes and perform using contrasting dynamics.
- *Appreciating* – describe and evaluate the influence of the Martial Arts on the style of the dance.

Music for the Dance

Instrumental music with an oriental/Eastern influence, e.g. '*The Killing Fields*' by Mike Oldfield.

**VIDEO
TITLE**

Gift of Tradition

Synopsis

This documentary video, produced in 1992, shows the various South Asian dance traditions which are present in Birmingham. It provides extracts of different dance styles which are explained on the video and explored in greater depth in the accompanying written resource notes:

'Showing dancers, teaching and performing at local venues, the video aims to broaden awareness of the educational and cultural values of South Asian dance, and to show an art form which has survived the passage of time and place.'

SAMPAD – Gift of Tradition

Dance Content (running order as on the video)

Classical Dance

1. *Kathak* dance from Northern India is performed as a duet. Danced by a man and a woman it demonstrates the intricate foot rhythms, swift turns and fluent gestures which are particular to this style. Also shown are the musicians playing a variety of traditional instruments.

2. *Bharata Natyam,* which was originally performed in the temples of Southern India, is shown and discussed by the dancer. There is also a piece based on a martial art form developed into a dance using swords and shields.

Folk Dance

Bhangra is shown in performance by a group of young men. This dance style has grown in popularity throughout Britain, largely because of the lively rhythmic music which accompanies the dance and the highly energetic movements designed to impress the audience with their strength and agility. Originally a male dance form, it can now be performed by either sex. As a harvest dance originating in the Punjab, it illustrates some of the work actions associated with this lifestyle but is now developing to create a new vocabulary which reflects the influence of western pop and disco dance styles on Bhangra.

The **resource pack** which can be purchased to accompany this video provides fuller and more detailed information on these dance styles and others not shown on the video. It also includes useful material on the interrelationship of dance with other South Asian art forms and a comprehensive resource list.

Characteristics of Kathak Dance

1. Top half of the body gracefully poised, often with one arm outstretched and the other bent across the body.

2. Feet in parallel position demonstrating crisp, clear and rhythmic footwork which creates sound patterns on striking the floor. The use of numerous ankle bells also enhances the sounds.

3. Fluid movement of the arms, wrists and hands which contrasts with the control of the upper body.

4. Varied facial expressions and stylised hand gestures (Mudras) to create characters and tell a story.

An additional resource for Kathak dance is the 54 minute video produced by the ILEA titled *The Kathak Dance*. This provides detailed information on the history and development of this style, explaining the significance of the movements as they are performed by the dancers. In a section called Learning Kathak Dance the technical skills and expressive qualities required in performance are fully discussed and demonstrated.

Characteristics of Bharata Natyam Dance

1. Upright posture with legs and feet turned out.

2. Use of the arms, legs and body to create geometric shapes.

3. Hand gestures which emphasise the body shape.

4. Rhythmic footwork using the foot to strike the floor and also used in a flexed position.

Characteristics of Bhangra Dance

1. Movement which stresses the main counts in the bar, *1&2&3&4*, and which is emphasised by a strong downbeat towards the ground.

2. A powerful low body position from which the actions have a downward thrust.

3. Isolated shoulder movements which are emphasised by body and hand twists.

4. Strong, energetic movement of the upper body and high-energy knee bounces.

5. Performed in a joyous, celebratory style including claps and smiling faces.

Figure 4.5 Gift of Tradition. © Bill Cooper.

Figure 4.6 Gift of Tradition. © Bill Cooper.

Ideas for Dance Frameworks and Choreographic Tasks

Traditional Dance (Figures 4.5 and 4.6)

Style – Kathak or Bharata Natyam

1. Learn two or three dance step patterns from the video, e.g. pivot turns, stamping steps, extended leg gestures, upright stance with the feet turned out and knees bent or with feet in parallel and legs straight.

2. Describe the main features of the body shapes, use photographs as additional reference material. Select and refine three of the shapes. These could be:

   (a) developed through the use of transitions such as jumps and turns, varying the dynamic qualities, and/or

   (b) combined with one partner or in a trio in which the shapes are copied, or used to complement/contrast with one another

   (c) structured with elements of repetition, unison and canon included.

3. Create or learn some of the stylised hand gestures and arm positions demonstrated, the contrasting linear and curved lines could be emphasised.

4. Specific hand gestures (Mudras) could be copied and children could invent their own to help in telling a simple story.

Music for the Dance

● SAMPAD produce a tape of classical South Asian music (see Audio Resources Appendix, page 85).
● Recordings by Ravi Shankar.

Harvest Celebration

Style – Bhangra

1. Discuss work actions associated with the harvest in India and create a phrase which links two or three exaggerated actions together, e.g. sowing seeds and cutting crops.

2. Clap the rhythm of the music, accenting *1&2* and perform on the spot, in different directions, and whilst walking at chest height.

3. Learn two or three movements from the video, e.g. the up and down of the shoulders, deep knee bends, travelling jumps and step hop.

4. Create a small group dance using the idea of a harvest celebration.

Music for the Dance

● Popular bhangra dance music.

VIDEO TITLE

Houston Ballet. Ghost Dances

Choreographed by Christopher Bruce

Premier in 1981 by Ballet Rambert at the Bristol Theatre Royal, performed on the video by the Houston Ballet company.

Synopsis

Ghostdances is a 27 minute ballet for eleven dancers who are divided into two clear groups, 'the ghosts' and 'the dead'. The dance contains a variety of movement vocabulary influenced by folk and social dances, and this is blended with classical ballet and contemporary dance styles. The music consists of seven folk tunes by the Peruvian folk group Inti-Illimani, and it uses traditional ethnic instruments arranged by Nicholas Carr.

BBC Radio 4 'Kaleidoscope' Monday 12 October 1981

'The Ghost Dances were part of Indian culture, both North and South America. The ghosts that come on to the stage are the dead on their way to Heaven or Hell. I just saw it happening in a sort of rocky barren landscape, where the Ghost Dancers had hung around for millions of years, and lying on rocks, like lots of say, animal images. They'd become birds and lizards as well as men, as they sort of sit around in this space. The people that wander on are wandering, as it were, from Life into Death. It's like their last... remembrances, their last statements, before they go very proudly at the end, to Death.'

(Christopher Bruce)

The Dance Idea

Its inspiration comes from two sources: a recording of some Peruvian ethnic songs, and Bruce's acquaintance with former dancer Joan Turner Jara. Jara is the widow of Chilean folksinger/actor/theatre director Victor Jara who was murdered in the 1973 coup against President Salvador Allende.

The programme note for the ballet is written by Christopher Bruce:

'I made this ballet for the innocent people of South America who from the time of the Spanish Conquests have been continuously devastated by political oppression.'

Bruce became increasingly interested in South America, especially the political situation and the upheavals that resulted. To him Latin America seemed a little bit like Ireland due to the disruption and pain experienced over many years of unrest:

'Although it has a South American setting, it's a universal story. You could parallel it with Poland or Afghanistan: cruelty, lack of human rights, people who suffer. So in a sense, it's indirectly political, but it's very much about humanity and just about how people get caught up, suffer and die.'

(22 May 1988, *Houston Post*)

Bruce researched into South American Indian rites and discovered tales of certain tribes who ground up the bones of dead, cremated children, made them into soup and drank it to symbolise the spiritual continuation of life. He also discovered that the dancers wore skull masks when they celebrated these rites.

'And so, I created three spirits, death spirits who are like three giant condors. And although they're quite frightening in their masks, they are for me quite objective spirits; they just symbolise death.'

(22 May 1988, *Houston Post*)

He also draws links to the Underworld of Greek mythology and talks of bringing 'the dead' into a stopping-off place, a resting place before they are carried on into the Underworld. As they pause in this place they recall certain moments from their lives, happy, sad or frightening, which are always quite brutally broken up or stopped:

'By the end, you've knocked these people down, down, again and again. But they always proudly rise up and carry on. There is a kind of dignity to the way they finally pass on to where they're going. And the ghost dancers, the spirits who are always waiting in this lonely place, take up their positions again to wait for the next group, because, you know, this is a continuing situation....'

(22 May 1988, *Houston Post*)

Notwithstanding the possible associations with events in Latin America, Bruce feels that his treatment of the subject has enough ambiguity to admit a variety of interpretations. He describes ballet as having not a specific one-line narrative but layers of ideas and images which form a collage and leave room for the audience's imagination to work.

What the critics say:

'Ghost Dances is wrenching and human.... With its folk rhythms, honest choreography and unsentimental humanism,....'

(Ann Sieber, 29 September 1994, *Houston Press*)

The music

'The more I listened to it, the more I fell in love with it. They're very simple tunes, very often melancholy and deeply evocative.'

(Bruce, 22 May 1988, *Houston Post*)

The South American folk music calls for the special sound of primitive ethnic instruments, and musicians who can play them. Rather than use a taped copy of the original recording from the British premier, Houston Ballet decided to use the transcribed music and play it live. In order to achieve this challenging task the musical director consulted several musical encyclopaedias to learn more about the exotic, strange-named instruments. In one instance he was able to use a modern bass guitar as its sound closely approximated to that heard on the original recording. Two contrasting guitars were also required, one with a classical technique, the other with flamenco technique. Many of the other instruments have strange and interesting names:

- The *quena* (sometimes spelt *kena,* or called *quena-quena* or *kena-kena*) is a breathy flute-like instrument that South Americans made of bone or wood.
- The *charango* is a small primitive lute.
- The *panpipes,* which have a double row of bamboo pipes.

Dance Content (running order as on the video)

Section 1

The three ghosts start to move in silence, creating a strange and haunting dance. Gradually the music is introduced and their dance develops into a powerful trio, whilst the 'dead' slowly enter at the back of the stage.

Section 2

Three men and three women perform a lively group dance but this is interrupted by the ghosts who leave the men lying on the floor as they dance with the women.

Section 3

In this duet the man and woman dance lovingly together until the man is agonisingly killed by two ghosts.

Section 4

A solo male dancer performs with four of the women to create a light-hearted and playful dance. Once again the ghosts interrupt and the man is led away.

Section 5

This duet is referred to as the little lama dance, as the man represents a lama who is being teased by his girlfriend. The happy and playful mood is destroyed as the girl is stricken by a ghost, leaving her boyfriend to hold her limp body in his arms.

Section 6

This section involves the eight dancers, who represent the dead, all dancing together expressing a lively and defiant mood. They echo previous motifs and repeat familiar groupings from earlier sections.

This piece ends with dancers in stillness, the ghosts slowly walk through them and as the opening music is repeated the 'dead' leave together and the ghosts re-inhabit the space.

Discussion and Video Analysis – The Ghosts

Watch the opening section of the dance where the three 'ghosts' perform together.

Movement Content

1. Describe the strange powerful dynamic qualities that they use.

2. Identify some of the action content such as:
- isolated movement of body parts, particularly the head
- inward movements across the body
- elbows leading the arm gestures
- reaching, dropping and rolling actions

– held body shapes
– contrasting arm gestures which are wide and extended, suggesting images of predatory birds.

3. *Analyse their use of space, which includes:*
– individually using the whole space
– levels from high to low
– dancing in a line.

4. *Comment on their overall style of movement:*
– unnatural movement
– powerful and athletic
– at times disjointed
– contrasts with flowing movement
– sudden changes of focus.

Use Figure 4.7 to reinforce these points, stress the clarity of body shape and the strength demonstrated in the pose of the 'ghost'.

Figure 4.7 Ghost Dances. © Jack Mitchell.

Costume

This is designed to convey the image of a skeleton with highlighted muscle definition. The skull masks have hollow eyes, no flesh and exaggerated teeth. The long, straggling hair emphasises the jerky, isolated head movements which are a characteristic part of their dance. They look human but seem to be associated with death and some sort of 'other' world.

Music

The same music is used for the 'ghosts' in the first and final sections of the dance. It has an eerie and haunting quality, characterised by a breathy pipe instrument and clear drum beat. They dance to the tempo of the music, which is quite slow and repetitive. As it repeats it becomes faster and louder. The music and movement together create an unreal and slightly ominous mood to the dance which builds in intensity.

Simple Dance of the 'Ghosts' Framework

A trio	Teaching points
A Walk into the space using strong, slow steps. Add isolated, sudden movements of the head and shoulders and arms. Make clear floor patterns. Develop the walk to include a held balance, use the clear body shapes shown on the video. Perform two or three times with the dancers moving and holding stillness at different times.	Emphasise a clear sense of focus and sudden changes of direction. Stress the control and body tension needed.
B Create a movement motif, use three actions from reach, drop, roll, turn, gesture. Emphasise the slightly unnatural, inward nature of the movement style. Perform the motif several times about the space, each of the three dancers dancing individually: • dance separately, using one motif or • dance in unison or • create three different motifs and perform them all	Include changes in level and fluent transitions. The motif should have a clear start and finish
C Use the large open arm-gestures, like the wings of the condor, as a transition to bring the three dancers in a line.	Use the video to copy the shapes.
D Create a chain dance, facing the front using some of the ideas on the video: • linking arms, touching shoulders • dropping slowly down onto one knee and then the other • copying the cross over step • turning to face sideways and taking slow, deliberate steps Perform as a trio in unison – finish in a strong, bold group shape	Stress the strength and power of the group dancing in unison.

More experienced dancers

- Repeat C.
- Repeat B, vary and develop the motif through:
  - changing the order of the movements
  - adding more travel
  - using different body parts.
- Finish by repeating A and ending in a strong, bold group shape.

Simple Dance

Learning Outcomes

Children should be guided to:
- *Composing* – Create a motif using expressive dynamic and spatial features.
- *Performing*:
  - Show clear body shapes and fluent transitions between the movements.
  - Show ability to listen and respond to the music.
- *Appreciating* – Describe how the three dancers achieve a feeling of strength and power through their movement and group relationships.

Figure 4.8 Ghost Dance © Bill Cooper.

More Experienced Dancers

Learning Outcomes

Children should be guided to:
- *Composing:*
  - Create and develop a motif with an understanding of how the dynamic and spatial features enhance expression.
  - Link the sections to make a whole dance.
- *Performing* – Attend to the expressive significance of the dynamics, spatial patterns and trio relationships.
- *Appreciating* – Discuss the overall form of the dance, including the use of repetition and development.

Music for the Dance

- The original music is available on CD.
- Instrumental panpipes music would be suitable if the rhythm was stressed.
- Peruvian folk music.

Discussion and Video Analysis – Folk Dance

Watch the group dances, Sections 2 and 6 on the video.

Movement Content

- Identify some of the action content such as:
  - walks
  - simple runs, legs lifted at the back
  - step patterns, e.g. (i) a one and two rhythm, stepping right–left–right with the accent on the first beat, (ii) the opening drop step in dance number 6
  - turns, using walks, running steps, pivoting on one foot or jumping.

- Analyse the group formations:
  - lines, two lines of three or one line of six
  - circle
  - chain, join hands, or one hand on the shoulder
  - front and back lines of three dancers, back line travels forward and through the front line
  - duets.

- Comment on their overall style of movement:
  - the dynamics include a range of quick, light and bouncy qualities, these contrast with the heavier, downward feel in some of the movements
  - it demonstrates characteristics of traditional folk dance, such as simple steps and changing group patterns.

Costume

It is designed to convey a range of everyday people who have fallen on hard and difficult times. Although some of the costumes are torn and ragged, there is a sense of dignity and pride in their appearance.

Music

Both of the group dances use lively, traditional South American tunes.

Folk Dance Framework

A dance for six dancers.
- Enter the performing space as a group of six, use simple walks or runs:
  1. Two lines of three.
  2. One line or chain of six.
  3. In pairs, holding hands.
  Finish in a line, two lines or a circle.

- Create a simple travelling step, using ideas taken from the action content. Use this to change the group formation two or three times.
- Teach the set drop step taken from dance number 6, perform in:
    1. One line of six in unison.
    2. Two lines of three, one behind the other in unison.
    3. Two lines of three, going in opposite directions.
    4. Two lines, front line dance the set step, back line choose a contrasting step, e.g. pivot turn, travelling in a chain. Lines change over using clear floor patterns and fluent steps.
- Repeat and/or develop the simple travel step and create a chain dance.
- Create an ending, decide whether to remain on or off stage.

Additional Ideas for More Experienced Dancers

- Include duets: three couples create their own duet, they could be performed at the same time *or* individually, while the other four dancers repeat a simple step in the background *or* they all perform the same duet, which would be danced as three couples at the same time, or as a couple separately.
- Create individual solo motifs, as shown towards the end of dance number 6. Extend and develop the movement vocabulary through copying and adapting the action content.

Teaching Points

- Stress the folk dance qualities, particularly the use of contrasting rhythmic steps and changing floor patterns.
- Encourage an awareness of dancing together to create a feeling of community strength and unity.

Learning Outcomes

Children should be guided to:
- *Composing* – Use a range of learned dance steps, figures and patterns to compose their own arrangements.
- *Performing* – Remember the changing patterns and perform the dance with an understanding of rhythm and a sense of style.
- *Appreciating* – The interrelationship between the dancers and their use of space to create patterns.

Music for the Dance

- The original music is available on CD (see Audio Resources Appendix, page 85).
- Instrumental music or folk songs from South America or Europe would be suitable, depending upon the setting for the dance.

Evaluation and Appreciation

Bruce creates a sense of unity and coherence through a range of choreographic devices which he deploys to avoid the dance appearing fragmented or disjointed. The following questions examine how he achieves this.

1. How do the three 'ghosts' help to provide continuity throughout the dance?

(a) The three 'ghosts' are present on stage when the dance begins and ends, and their presence is continuous throughout.

(b) They bring each section (except 6) to an end by killing the people or receiving their bodies.

(c) The use of repetition with slight variation is a device employed when the 'ghosts' threaten or kill and take the dancers. Who they take and their method of taking varies, also the number of 'ghosts' involved and the nature of the death or degree of violence.

2. As the set, props and costume remain constant throughout, how does the choreographer achieve changes in time, mood and atmosphere?

Changes are achieved through the use of:

(a) lighting

(b) grouping, with different numbers of dancers performing

(c) movement content, see the video analysis notes on the 'ghosts' and the folk dance.

3. Once they enter the dancers are continuously present on stage. What effect does this have on the atmosphere?

(a) The 'ghosts' continuous presence, in the space and on the rocks, suggests that this is their habitat. Although they sometimes perform individually their malevolent intention is always the same and at times they dance in unison creating a feeling of power and unity.

(b) The 'dead' enter and exit as a group, passing through the stage space during the course of the dance from stage left to stage right. This suggests that they are on a journey and their time in this strange place or underworld is merely a transition from one state to another. Once on stage they all remain and thus they can be identified as a group or community.

4. In every dance with 'the dead' there are two themes or contrasting moods. Describe these and discuss what ideas they might convey.

The two themes or moods might be summarised as feeling 'alive' or 'dead and lifeless'. When 'alive' the movement content is based on wordly human relationships and is frequently lively and playful, taking the style of a folk dance. They are seen to be recalling some aspect of everyday life as normal people and reliving their happy memories.

When 'dead' they appear as lost beings, devoid of human relationship and warmth, and lacking in purpose and energy. This reflects the oppression and suffering they have endured. Although the balance between these two aspects shifts in each section the contrasting moods are ever present providing interest and tension throughout the work.

5. How is music/sound used to link the separate dances?

Each dance is set to a distinct piece of music; however, they are all linked by a mixture of faint instrumental sounds, howling wind and silence.

VIDEO TITLE

Late Flowering Lust

Choreographed by Matthew Bourne

Premier in 1994 by Adventures in Motion Pictures, a production for BBC television, running time 53 minutes.

Synopsis

The production is set during the pre-war era at a weekend house party in the Home Counties and is centred around the poetry of John Betjeman. The dance is incorporated into the work demonstrating a variety of ideas and moods which illustrate the poems.

'... it features a superb central performance from actor Nigel Hawthorne.'

'The soundtrack is an internal monologue that juxtaposes a dozen, often ironic love poems by John Betjeman with Jim Parker's clever pastiche of twentieth century popular music. The action takes place during a country-house weekend, with the AMP dancers playing a charming but self-centred clique of sleek Oxbridge types. They virtually ignore Hawthorne, and certainly fail to recognise any of his quiet desperation.'

(*Dance Now*, **4** (**3**) 1995)

Figure 4.9 Late Flowering Lust: the Tennis Dance. © Gabrielle Crawford

Dance Content

Matthew Bourne deftly exploits the comic potential in many of the dance ideas he develops in this work. These include (running order as on the video):

- *Section 1* – A short extract of Morris Dance, with dancers in full costume.
- *Section 2* – A light-hearted and energetic Keep Fit dance.
- *Section 3* – Three dances which use sporting actions as the starting point for their movement vocabulary:
   (i)   golf
   (ii)   tennis – *see the Frameworks*
   (iii)   swimming.
- *Section 4* – A short extract of romantic duets.
- *Section 5* – A lively group piece deploying the social dance styles of the 1930s, including the Turkey Trot and Charleston – *see the Framework.*

Discussion and Video Analysis – The Tennis Dance

1. What is the starting point for the dance idea?
The literal actions of tennis, a sport played mainly by the more affluent in society in pre-war times.

2. How does the choreographer develop the actions to make them more dance like?
The choreographer:
- exaggerates and enlarges the literal actions
- develops and varies the movement through adding jumps, turns and gestures
- repeats movements several times
- rhythmically patterns the movement
- creates phrases and sequences of movement
- incorporates different levels to give variety.

3. How do the dancers create the illusion of playing with a real ball?
Through the use of focus and awareness of body tension. The tennis rackets are also used to suggest contact with a ball.

4. Use descriptive language to describe how the dancers move; select from the following wordbank: sudden, darting, leaping, flowing, balanced, off balance – and add words of your own.
Appropriate words from those suggested, plus other suitable descriptive language, including metaphors and similes.

5. What feelings do the dancers convey and how are they shown? Give particular examples, e.g. staring straight ahead to show concentration.

Encourage the association of feelings to particular movements in the dance.

Tennis Dance – A Simple Dance Framework

A duet	Teaching points
A Individually use a running step to (1) run on the spot or (2) travel into a space or (3) travel into the space creating a simple floor pattern	Emphasise an upright posture, exaggerated knee lift and pointed toes.
B Teach a set step from the video, use the extract where the dancers are on the steps and move in to the low get ready position (1) jump to the right side and back to the left or (2) add jumping backwards and forwards.	Stress changes of level and clarity of direction
C Choose two still poses suggesting a tennis action (Figure 4.9); these could be taken from the video or the children could create their own. Perform them one after the other, holding each clearly for several counts. Repeat two or three times. Repeat A travelling to meet a partner. Facing each other: (1) repeat B and/or (2) repeat C using question and answer, i.e. dancer 1 moves and holds their pose, dancer 2 moves and holds their pose.	Encourage the use of body tension for balance and the importance of focus.
D Individually create a simple action phrase using the tennis strokes as a starting point. Link the literal tennis movements with a jump, a turn, a roll or a gesture. Suggest holding moments of stillness at the end or during the phrase.	Encourage simple contrasts in levels and fluency of movement
E Hold a finishing position to show winning/losing. Finish the dance: (1) run to meet your partner and shake hands or (2) run off court together/separately	Exaggerate the gestures.

Learning Outcomes

Children should be guided to:

- *Composing* – pattern their movements in space and create simple action phrases, with an awareness of a partner.
- *Performing* – show clarity of movement in action and space, using the dynamic qualities to enrich their expressive ideas.
- *Appreciating* – describe and interpret how the use of action, space and dynamics suggests meaning in dance.

Tennis Dance for More Experienced Dancers

A dance for four	Teaching points
A In two's create a running phrase which travels into the performance space; include: 1. Changes of direction, forward, backwards and sideways. 2. Movements on the spot.	Emphasise an upright posture, posture, exaggerated knee lift and pointed toes plus clarity of direction.
B Individually create a 'warm-up' using rhythmic repeated patterns of movement, e.g. knee bends, side stretches, using different levels.	Stress clarity of exaggerated actions.
C In two's select three still poses suggesting a tennis action, these could be copied from the video or the children could create their own. Perform them: 1. in unison, copying each other or 2. vary the time each pose is held, e.g. 4 counts, 2 counts	Sensitivity to partner and design of the two bodies in space.
D In four's use the content from C to choreograph a repetitive sequence of poses; include the use of: 1. action/reaction or 2. contrasting/complementary shapes or 3. variations in timing	Encourage awareness of the overall design and the inter-relationship of the four dancers.
E Teach an action phrase as a set study using movements from the video and your own ideas – perform in unison as a whole class.	Encourage accuracy of action, space and dynamics.
F Either: 1. use the study and rearrange it spatially to create the illusion of a tennis game or 2. vary and develop the set study to create the illusion of a tennis game. Finish the dance – decide on a group ending and exit from the performing space.	Highlight the spatial patterns and dynamic variations. A convincing and effective ending is important, try to explore a variety of different resolutions to the dance.

Learning Outcomes

Children should be guided to:

- *Composing* – Demonstrate understanding of group relationships and formal devices: repetition, development and contrast
- *Performing* – Perform accurately and fluently, attending to the expressive significance of dynamics, spatial patterns and relationships.
- *Appreciating* – Evaluate and discuss the overall structure of the dance recognising the use of compositional devices.

1930s Social Dance – Ideas for Dance Frameworks and Choreographic Tasks

A dance for 6–8 dancers:

1. Create a party scene, props could be used such as chairs, tables to give variety in levels.
2. Using the foot tapping and simple hand gestures, gradually involve all the dancers in a simple rhythmic pattern:
   (a) create question and answer phrases as if in conversation at a party *or*
   (b) dancers could change positions in the group, hold moments of stillness *or*
   (c) exaggerate gestures using stylised movements.
3. In two's create a simple sequence using the Charleston steps and variations shown on the video. Repeat and change partners in succession.
4. As a group, create a motif based on the hand jive gestures:
   (a) learn from the video *or*
   (b) create own variations.
5. Teach a study based on the Turkey Trot line dance (Figure 4.10), include the head-to-head and elbow movements. Choreography could include:
   (a) lines travelling in opposite directions
   (b) unison and canon.
6. Repeat any of the sections.
7. Create a lively uplifting finish to the dance.

Teaching Points

- Stress the *stylistic* features of the dance, particularly the use of relaxed, rhythmic gestures and step patterns.
- Encourage the use of exaggerated, theatrical expressive qualities to capture the gaiety of the mood.
- Look at the choreographers' staging of the dance, the effective use of changing group relationships and props to add visual interest.

Learning Outcomes

Children should be guided to:

- *Composing* – Develop dance phrases through repeating them in time and space and rearranging group relationships.
- *Performing* – Dance expressively in order to communicate the idea using stylistically defined movement.
- *Appreciating* – Discuss the appropriateness and originality of movement content to convey the dance idea in their own/others/professional choreography.

Music for the Dances

- Lively instrumental music of the 1930s.
- The poetry of Betjeman with musical accompaniment is available on CD (see Audio Resources Appendix, page 85).

Figure 4.10 1930s Social Dance: the Turkey Trot Dance. © Bill Cooper.

L'Enfant et les Sortilèges

Choreographed by Jiri Kylian.

Performed by Netherlands Dance Theatre.

Synopsis

The dance centres upon a naughty little boy of about 7 years old who refuses to do his school work. His mother reprimands him and confines him to the room. In his anger he vandalises his books and the furniture, but magic happens and the room comes to life. Objects such as the chairs and the grandfather clock seek their revenge upon him, the fire threatens him and he is very frightened. The boy even encounters a terrifying teacher of mathematics who puts him through mental anguish. In despair he flees into the garden but the animals attack him, fierce cats, frogs and moths torment the boy. In the turmoil a squirrel is injured and the child, realising he has been cruel and misbehaved, binds the squirrel's injured paw. This act of kindness is a turning point and the animals allow him to return to his mother, for whom he has been calling. The boy falls asleep in her arms, 'with a new understanding of the world around him'. (Video notes, RM Arts '86). In his introduction to the dance Kylian explains: 'I would love if the audience who sees this work feels like someone who is looking into a child's book that is lost for a long time'.

The story and the characters certainly have a fairytale quality where magic makes anything possible and kindness conquers anger and cruelty. The music is by Maurice Ravel with a libretto sung in French which informs the storyline.

Dance Content (running order as on the video)

The dance follows the little boy's encounters with different animals and objects. The fantastic set is designed with dancers inside oversized furniture and wearing exaggerated costumes.

Section 1

The bored and angry little boy vents his frustration in a temper tantrum, striking out at the furniture and teasing the cats.

Section 2

In this section:

(a) two chairs dance together

(b) there is a clashing and striking clock dance

(c) a teapot and cup perform a duet.

Section 3

The fire leaps out at the boy and the two dancers dart and jump menacingly around him, fiercely manipulating his body and gesticulating at him.

Section 4

A shepherd and shepherdess perform a tender and touching duet, using their long crooks as props. At times this has a medieval dance like quality as a tambor sets the rhythm and pipes play.

Section 5

The princess, whom the boy loves, and the prince dance a lyrical duet.

Section 6

A caricature of an irate mathematics teacher torments the little boy.

Section 7

In this section various animals are represented in dance sequences including

(a) two cats

(b) moths and a bat

(c) frogs.

Section 8

The dance concludes with the boy helping to release the squirrel from a cage and tending its wounds. As the animals acknowledge this act of kindness the cage becomes transformed into an outsize version of his mother's skirt and he clambers up it to fall asleep in her arms.

Dance Ideas

1. The feelings of the little boy at the start of the dance provide a rich stimulus for movement content and ideas which could be developed in a wider personal and social context (see Section 1, *Framework*).

2. In Section 3 the lively fire dance contains a variety of action content which could inspire children to create their own work.

3. The animals each have a characteristic movement style and their movement sequences provide several dance ideas with contrasting action and dynamic qualities. (see Sections 2 and 7, *Framework*).

Discussion and Video Analysis

Section 1

The stimulus for a dance about **moods** and **feelings**. Watch the first few minutes of the work, until the mother enters (*see Framework*).

1. Discuss how the little boy *feels* during this extract. Ideas might include angry, cross, in a temper, frustrated, bored, furious. Create a wordbank of these associated feelings.

2. Relate these feelings to his *actions;* what does he do to let us know how he is feeling? For example:

(a) Drumming fingers and swinging legs to show boredom

(b) Rocking on the table to indicate frustration

(c) Slapping hands on the table and kicking out to show anger

(d) Pulling a face and tearing his hair to show he is in a temper.

3. Describe *how* he performs these movements, e.g. sudden, jerky, strong.

4. Discuss why he feels like this and encourage children to share what puts them in to a similar mood and how they vent their feelings. Can they associate their experiences with those of the little boy?

Section 7

The stimulus for an **animal dance**, focus on one or several of the creatures, identify their particular movement style (*see Framework*):

1. *What does the animal do?* For example, the cats curl and uncurl their whole body, stretch, leap and pounce, use their heads and hands in isolation.

2. *How do they move?* For example, the cats move smoothly, suddenly and slowly with an undulating, rippling quality.

Angry Dance Framework

Watch the opening section of the video starting with the angry little boy at the table.

A solo dance	Teaching points
A Teach a set sequence using a variety of movements from the video, e.g.: ● Sit on the floor, knees bent, head down, hit the floor with the palms of the hands x 4. ● In the sitting position rock R, L, R, L hitting the floor with alternate hands. ● Swing legs round to finish lying on tummy, copy the body shape the boy makes when he is on the table and 'pulling a face'. ● Run fingers through hair 4x, R, L, R, L, repeat having come to a kneeling position. ● Stand, clench tummy as on the video. ● Finish with a strong kick.	Decide on a rhythm pattern, this could be slow ↔ quick. Ensure the transitions between the actions are fluent. Emphasise the importance of facial expressions.
B Create a simple rhythmic stamping phrase which travels. Repeat this 2 or 3 times changing direction.	Stress strong dynamics, clenched fists, flexed feet and bent knees.
C Develop an action phrase using words as a stimulus, e.g. furious, cross, frustration, angry, temper. The movements could include run, jump, land and turn.	Encourage the expressive use of the words to accompany the movement. Ensure there is dynamic contrast within the phrase. Ideas could also be taken from the duet where the boy and his mother dance together.
D Further development – in two's create an action and and reaction sequence to suggest taunting or 'poking fun' at each other.	Use different body parts and stress clear, angular shapes. Include a change of level.

Learning Outcomes

Children should be guided to:
- *Composing* – Create an action phrase, using repetition and action and reaction.
- *Performing:*
  - Be able to perform basic body actions using strong, controlled movement
  - Show rhythmic awareness.
- *Appreciating* – Describe and interpret the expressive qualities in the video and in their own dances.

Music for the Dance

Rhythmic expressive word patterns could be used to accompany the dance, these may be performed 'live' or pre-recorded by the children.

Cat Dance Framework

Watch the opening of the video and the subsequent section where the little boy torments the cats.

A duet	Teaching points
A With a partner create a starting position, use contact and rounded body shapes. Improvise a phrase of movement using different body parts and exaggerated gestures e.g. back, head, hand, foot, to suggest waking up and slowly stretching. Develop the idea to move under, over and around each other.	Emphasise fluent, sinuous movements. Stress awareness of partner's movement and use of space.
B In two's create a teasing, playful duet; ideas could include: • run and jump, showing off leaping skills, • jump over each other • pounce and land in a roll on the floor • dodge from side to side of each other.	Try to copy the body shapes used in the jumps on the video, e.g. sharp and spiky, curved or stretched.
C Ending – repeat parts of A to finish in a complementary body shape.	Discuss the transition from B, which is fast and lively, to the calm and restful mood to finish the dance

Learning Outcomes

Children should be guided to
- *Composing* – Develop the ability to improvise and dance with an awareness of a partner.
- *Performing* – Use the whole body and body parts to show fluidity of movement.
- *Appreciating* – Identify how literal cat movements can be exaggerated and represented in a dance.

Random Dance Company. Anarkos

Choreographer Wayne McGregor.

Performed by Random Dance Company in 1995 at The Place, as part of the Spring Re-Loaded II season of dance.

Synopsis

This contemporary dance work uses highly charged and energetic movement material to express ideas associated with anarchy and chaos.

Following the performance, which was filmed live at The Place, McGregor discusses how he worked on the piece. Although his starting point was a novel the dance does not tell a story, rather he extracts information and contexts which could apply to contemporary culture. He draws on ideas of anarchy and chaos: 'working in movement to create, through highly ordered and structured material quite chaotic and random looking movement.'

McGregor explains how the themes of manipulation, competition and aspiration provide the inspiration for the vocabulary of the dance. The movement language which evolves stresses, 'isolating, movements which ricochet through the body' generating a sense of violence, even in the slower sections because of its dislocated qualities.

Throughout the work the dancers use physical contact, lifting and supporting one another with constantly changing relationships between the five dancers, two men and three women. The musical accompaniment uses computer-generated sounds to provide a varied and contemporary feel to the work. It explores the extremes of rhythm and makes reference to techno, ambient and jungle styles of music and has a driving, repetitive quality.

Dance Content (running order as on the video)

Section 1

A lively and energetic opening with the five dancers constantly moving on and off the stage space. The duets show the dancers reacting to one another's touch and initiating movement through contact with each other.

Section 2

In this slow and sustained section a dreamlike fantasy world is suggested. As the dancers lean on and support each other there is at times a feeling of dependency and caring but also a surreal sense of dislocation with no sense of purpose or focus.

The transition into the next section is in silence as 2 dancers perform a floorwork sequence including clear angular shapes and using constantly changing points of support.

Section 3

This section is another high-energy piece with lively jumps and turns but it also includes contrasting slower movement phrases.

Section 4

Another slow section with held balances and very sustained movement. It features a male duet with a variety of lifts and supporting positions.

The transition is again performed in silence as two women dance in unison, holding angular shapes and balances.

Section 5

The finalé is uptempo and energetic with references to the opening section. It is a culmination of the preceding movement content, demonstrating a range of dynamics and changing group relationships.

Discussion and Video Analysis

Extracts of the dance could be used to generate discussion and analysis of the features of this movement style and the choreographer's use of it to communicate his ideas.

Characteristics of the style include:

- Basic actions, such as jumps, rolls and lifts performed as phrases of movement.
- Transference of weight onto the floor using different body parts and with the use of a partner.
- Physical contact with another dancer, lifting, supporting, balancing, pushing and pulling each other.
- Travelling in contact with another dancer.
- Swinging movements which initiate action phrases.
- Constant changes of direction and level.
- Use of a wide and contrasting dynamic range, including rapid energetic sequences and sustained, slow-motion sections.
- Body parts moving in different directions.

Discussion of the ideas and feelings suggested by the different sections of the dance could provide a wordbank to stimulate movement. For example, 'crash', 'collide', 'fragment', and 'disintegrate', as words to imply chaos. In contrast some of the partner and solo work is more harmonious and supportive.

Additional Resources

The use of **photographs** and **visual images** could provide additional stimulus. These might include pictures of dancers in contact with each other, to extend the children's repertoire of ideas and suggest positions that they could copy and adapt. By looking at specific features the expressive qualities could be discussed, for example body shapes which are rounded suggest harmony and support whilst angular shapes may imply anger and tension; or a dancer standing over their partner at a higher level might create a feeling of dominance and power. A study of the comic art of Roy Liechtenstein which has titles such as 'Wall Explosion No.1' and 'Whaam!' would also provide strong visual images that could be translated into movement.

Ideas for Dance Frameworks and Choreographic Tasks

1. Runs which:
   (a) Change direction and speed using focus to provide a sense of urgency or disorder.
   (b) Lead to a collision with an imaginary wall and the rebound/collapse that follows.
   (c) Include simple jumps and turns.

2. Create an action phrase using three or four words from the wordbank generated in discussion, e.g., 'shatter', 'split' and 'wham' to suggest chaos. Repeat and vary the phrase using changes of direction and moments of stillness (view the fast sections, particularly 3 and 5, noting the use of slow motion to emphasise movements).

3. Partner work:
   (a) 'help your partner up from the floor', encourage the use of contact with different body parts. As A is helped up B drops down to the floor and vice versa, developing into an action/reaction sequence. Emphasise the rhythm and fluency. What is the required feeling between the two people?
   (b) Using ideas from the video or taken from photographs explore ideas of support and weight bearing. Create a sequence linking two or three ideas together. Experiment with using travel, such as walks and runs, into a lift or supported position. Does this section suggest a different relationship between the two people? (View Sections 2 and 4.)

4. Using the video create a set study which the children learn. This could be a simple motif which they can they repeat, vary and develop.

5. The transitions contain moments of stillness with the dancers in clear body shapes, particularly on the floor. These could be drawn and copied to create an individual sequence, this could be taught to a partner and danced in unison as on the video.
(See page 81 for safety procedures.)

Music for the Dance

- Popular music, ambient, techno and jungle styles.
- Brian Eno recordings.
- Minimalistic composers, e.g. Steve Reich, Philip Glass, Michael Nyman.

'Still Life' at the Penguin Café

Choreographed by David Bintley.

Premier in 1988 by the Royal Ballet.

Synopsis

The ballet takes the issue of man's destruction of the natural environment, looking particularly at animals in danger of extinction. Bintley creates a dance for each of the endangered species, including a Longhorned Ram, a Kangaroo Rat, a Flea, a Zebra and of course the Penguins. Towards the end of the ballet there is a 'Carnival celebration dance' for everyone. This, however, comes to an abrupt end as distant gunfire is heard, resulting in panic and confusion. The piece concludes as the animals move off in pairs and are seen safely inside an ark:

The Great Auk, a native of the Atlantic, was the original penguin ('white-head' in Welsh) – the penguins of the Southern Hemisphere having derived their name from European sailors who saw the similarity.

The numbers of Great Auks were already diminishing rapidly by the beginning of the nineteenth century as the result of reckless persecution by man. Continued hunting and natural disasters finally wiped them out completely. On 3 June 1844, on the Island of Eldey, off the coast of Iceland, three fishermen discovered the last two living Great Auks. They were a breeding pair with a single egg. Jon Brandsson and Sigourer Isleffson killed the two adult birds with clubs while Ketil Ketilsson smashed the egg with his boot.
David Bintley, based on the *Doomesday Book of Animals* by David Day (Ebury Press, 1981)

The music is by the Penguin Café Orchestra, composed by Simon Jeffes, and consists of eight selected pieces.

Royal Ballet Education notes – Simon Jeffes and the Penguin Café

'What sort of music is it? Ideally I suppose it's the sort of music you want to hear, music that will lift your spirit. It's the sort of music played by imagined wild, free, mountain people creating sounds of a subtle dreamlike quality. It is café music, but café in the sense of a place where people's spirits communicate and mingle, a place where music is played that often touches the heart of the listener. Originally I created the Penguin Café Orchestra to make such music. I wrote for violin, cello, guitar and piano but I use whatever instruments I have...'

(Simon Jeffes)

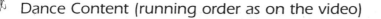

Dance Content (running order as on the video)

Section 1

Penguins dance as waiters, weaving in and out of each other balancing trays of drinks. This develops into an elegant large-scale social dance scene set in the Penguin Café.

Section 2

The Longhorned Ram is performed by a woman who dances with a group of men who gracefully lift and support her.

Section 3

The Kangaroo Rat performs a lively and energetic dance which suggests his origins from the 'backwoods' of America through his costume of baggy dungarees and country dance style of movement.

Section 4

The Flea dances with a group of Morris men in an amusing and light-hearted manner.

Section 5

The Cape Zebra performs a dance which includes African influences, such as low shuffling steps and jumps, and isolated gestures. The women wear striking black and white costumes which suggest zebra skin. They appear oblivious to the zebra who is about to die and use stylised repetitive gestures to suggest disdain and arrogance.

Section 6

A family of three Rainforest people perform a wistful dance, reflecting on the destruction of the natural environment.

Section 7

A carnival celebration led by a Brazilian Monkey brings all the characters together in a joyful dance.

Section 8

A storm breaks out giving rise to fear and confusion. Eventually the animals are seen travelling in two's into an ark and the ballet finishes with a still tableau, the animals safe inside the ark.

Dance Ideas

- A variety of dances inspired by different animals represented in the ballet, particularly the penguins, zebra or monkey.
- The attitude of people towards the animals, such as the women who arrogantly wear the

fur and animal skins as items of fashion during the zebra dance.
- A dance which develops the idea of carnival and celebration. This could then be contrasted with the panic and confusion that ensues as gunfire is heard and a storm breaks.
- A Morris style dance – see the *Framework*.
- A 'Hoedown' or 'Barndance' – see the *Frameworks*.

Discussion and Video Analysis – Morris Dance

Watch the complete Morris Dance with the 'Flea', focusing mainly on the Morris men (Section 4 on the video). Discuss the *movement content, floor patterns,* and *style of the piece.*

1. Movement Content

Identify the different steps they use such as:
- skips
- jumps with two feet
- hops
- leap-frog

2. Floor Patterns

Describe and/or draw the different floor patterns they create. These include:
- A circle
- A circle, with three dancers dancing anti-clockwise and the rest dancing clockwise weaving in and out of each other
- Lines across the space   x x x x x   and up and down the space   x
                                                                     x
                                                                     x

  or facing a partner   x x
                            x x
                            x x
- Casting off from two lines   x   x
                                   x   x
                                 ↖ x   x ↗
- A knot, where the dancers finish entangled in each others arms!

3. Style

Comment on the overall style of the movement:
- Performed with an upright stance.
- Bouncy and well co-ordinated movement.
- Feet can be relaxed or flexed for certain steps.

Costume

A combination of characteristic and traditional Morris dance costume is worn by the men. They wear a hat with ribbons, a white shirt with crossed baldricks, britches with braiding, a

sash, and long white socks. The use of sticks is a familiar prop and handkerchiefs were also often employed as an important visual effect in the dance.

Music

The original title given to the piece by the composer Simon Jeffes was *'Pythagoras's trousers'* but Bintley has changed it to *'The Ecstasy of Dancing Fleas'*. It is a repetitive, rhythmic piece with a light and bouncy quality to suit the dance style.

Morris Dance

The Morris has a very ancient history, more ancient than even the fifteenth and sixteenth Century references to it in church records. Attempts to discover the original source remain inconclusive. However, links between the Spanish and English courts in the fourteenth century are said to have provided the basis for Morris Dance. The style we have today started about 1650 and traditionally uses six dancers, i.e. three couples. It has survived suppression at various stages in history but thanks to the work of several dedicated people, particularly of Cecil Sharp in this century, many of the dances have been recovered and recorded. He visited numerous villages across England to find old dancers and learn from them the tunes, steps and figures of their dances and then taught them to others. By means of the English Folk Dance Society, which he founded in 1911, he then spread this knowledge and practical expertise.

It has always been a performance style of dance with both men and women dancing. The idea that only men should participate started quite recently in the 1930s. Traditionally it is related to the church and May Day celebrations, being seen as a break in the agricultural cycle of work. Dancers were often paid to perform and were well respected. However, its relationship with patronage required large socially structured communities and in Victorian times it began to disappear, as it was perceived as too rowdy and leisure pursuits were frowned upon.

The end of the 1960s saw a resurgence of folk culture and Morris once again flourished and continues to develop. There are many different varieties depending upon the village of origin but the type of music and manner of performance makes the style identifiable. The music generally features instruments favoured in earlier times including the pipe and tabor, the fiddle and the concertina or accordion. It relies strongly on complex rhythm patterns and a clear melody to give it its characteristic qualities. (See Peck (1978)).

Traditional Morris Dance – A Simple Framework

A dance for six people	Teaching points
A Skip into the performing space, one behind the other, to form a circle. Skip round in a circle. Learn the following step from the video: ● On the spot, 3 skips clockwise (R) followed by a jump, 2 feet to 2 feet. Repeat. ● Repeat the phrase 2 times turning anticlockwise (L)	Accentuate the knee lift. Encourage high, bouncy jumps.
B Turn to face a partner in the circle. 3 dancers should face clockwise and 3 dancers should face anticlockwise. Starting with the R hand pass partner, using a skipping step. Meet the next dancer and use the L hand to pass them. Continue the pattern until the dancers are back where they started from.	Make sure the dancers all start with their R hand and pass R shoulders first. Walk the pattern through several times before dancing.
C Skip into one line across the space and hold hands, Copy the hopping step from the video: ● Hop R, hop L, hop R twice, shaking the leg to the side ● Repeat to the L. A simpler version of this would be 4 hops on the R, 4 hops on the L.	To start the step take off from two land on one foot, this co-ordination will need practice.
D Dancers lift arms to form a series of arches and the dancer at the front of the line leads the other dancers through the arches.	Decide on the leader, walk the pattern through carefully, make sure the dancers hold hands and the last dancer turns under their own arm.
E Skip back to the circle and repeat B	
F Skip into a line, one behind the other and repeat the hopping motif from C.	
G Dancers 1,3,5 cast off and skip to their L Dancers 2,4,6 cast off and skip to their R Create two lines X 6 5 X X 4 3 X X 2 1 X	It is important that each dancer skips to the front before casting off.
H Skip or run towards partner for 4 counts and: 1. Link R arms for 4 steps, then L arm for 4 steps and return to original place. 2. Clap R hands across for 4 and left hands across for 4, return to original place or across to the opposite side.	The claps can represent the sticks, or real sticks could be used. Some children may be able to perform the skip, jump and hit sticks as on the video
I Skip into a circle to finish the dance	

Learning Outcomes

Children should be guided to:

● *Composing* – Combine simple set steps and create formations and figures.
● *Performing* – Perform the steps accurately and with an awareness of the rhythm and phrasing of the music.
● *Appreciating* – Describe and name the dance steps, formations and figures they perform.

Additional Ideas for More Experienced Dancers

● For the basic *Morris step* the terms 'two-step' and 'four-step' are used to mean respectively the 'one, hop, two, hop' step and the 'one, two, three, hop' step. Although not shown in this video it could be taught to the children and used in the dance framework to replace some of the skipping steps.

> 'The change of foot, as well as the hop, is made with a slight spring, i.e. the weight of the body is raised from the ground before each step so that the change of foot takes place in the air...'
>
> (Maud Karpeles; in Bacon (1974))

● An additional dancer could take the role of the 'Flea' who might represent the 'Fool' in traditional Morris dance. She is constantly jumping and hopping from one foot to the other and being trapped or jumped over by the men.

Music for the Dance

● Traditional folk music.
● Penguin Café music as on the video, *'Pythagoras's Trousers'* is available on CD and tape.

(See Audio Resources Appendix, page 85)

Discussion and Video Analysis – The Texan Kangaroo Rat

Watch the dance (Section 3 on the video) and discuss the movement content, composition, and style of the piece.

Movement Content

1. The action content includes a variety of different travelling steps, including hops, jumps and gallops. These are varied to produce complex step patterns which also include turns and gestures. The exaggerated use of bent elbows and knees and flexed feet is also a feature. This is in contrast to the opening section which includes movements of isolated body parts and stillness.

2. The dancer travels in several different directions, forwards, backwards and sideways, using all of the stage space. There are changes of level as he drops to the floor and takes his weight on his hands and when he jumps high into the air.

3. The movement qualities are mainly light and bouncy, and it is danced with energy and vitality as he moves about the space. This contrasts with the opening and closing sections where the dancer is on the floor and uses sudden, quick movements and some more flexible actions to suggest waking up and falling asleep.

Composition

There is considerable use of repetition throughout the dance, particularly of step patterns and gestures. Variety is achieved through changing the spatial patterns and use of levels. Highlights include the jumps and the floorwork.

Style

Throughout the dance the exaggerated use of bent elbows and knees, and flexed feet suggests a style of movement associated with a 'Hoedown' or 'Barndance'. This is enhanced by the simple costume, of baggy dungarees and T-shirt, and the music which could be associated with an American Square dance or other types of country dancing.

Dance Framework for a 'Hoedown'

	Teaching points
A Create a still 'tableau' with the group of four dancers close together to suggest country life as hillbillies. Individually in canon each dancer performs a large, exaggerated gesture as though coming to life and then returns to their starting position. Gradually start to move using isolated body parts, e.g. foot tapping, fingerclicking, clapping, in time to the music.	Use levels and directions to add visual interest in the group shape or tableau.
B In two's gallop to the side of the space, ◄─x x ─► two travelling to the R and two to the L ◄─x x ─►	Exaggerate the use of bent knees and elbows.
C In two's create a step pattern which can be used to travel across the space; include: 1. a variety of simple steps, e.g. walks, gallops, heel and toe, polka, hops. 2. turns and arm gestures. Choreograph the dance so that two or three duos are travelling across at one time, whilst the others repeat their clapping or foot tapping at the sides of the space. Finish with the group of four in their original starting space.	Ideas may be taken from the video to increase the complexity of the steps or to suggest gestures. Stress that everyone is dancing the whole time, even when at the sides.
D Create a series of traditional folk dance figures and patterns, e.g. 1. R hand and L hand star. 2. Arming or turning with a partner. 3. Do-si-do. 4. Gallops in a circle.	Recall figures they may have learnt in traditional folkdances, still emphasise the 'hoedown' style which has a feeling of the weight going down and into the floor.
E Compose a motif selecting three or four of the shapes in Figures 4.11 – 4.14 and linking them together. This could be created by: 1. Each group of four working collectively to compose one motif. 2. Each individual in the group creating a motif and teaching it to the others, providing four motifs. 3. Everyone learning the same motif designed by one group or one person. Through the use of unison and canon this section could be extended and varied.	Emphasise the need to copy the body shapes shown in the photographs accurately. They may be repeated several times in the motif and interesting transitions between each shape should be encouraged.
F Finish the dance: 1. Decide whether to repeat an earlier section such as C or D. 2. Choose how to end, e.g. everyone back in their original starting positions, a whole group 'tableau' or with just one group still 'on stage' dancing until they drop!	

Figure 4.11–4.14 Hoedown: dance framework. © Bill Cooper

Learning Outcomes

Children should be guided to:

- *Composing* – create a motif and understand the use of unison and canon in their dances.
- *Performing* – perform with clarity and style, perform sequences of movement demonstrating co-ordination and a sense of rhythm.
- *Appreciating* – identify the characteristics of this style of dance.

Music for the Dance

- Traditional lively folk music.
- Cajun music with a 'hillbilly' feel.

A Simple Framework based on the Texan Kangaroo Rat Dance

This dance explores the animal-like movements as well as the 'hoedown' style of the piece. Listen to the music and identify phrases which suggest the start or finish of a dance section.

A duet	Teaching points
A Individually start in a small body shape on the floor. Gradually wake up, using movements of isolated body parts, e.g. arms, feet, head.	Encourage the clear use of individual body parts.
B Find a partner and in two's gallop about the space, finish in a space.	
C A sit and watch B perform, B can copy one or 2 of the pictures (Figures 4.11–4.14) and dance them on the spot to show how clever they are B sit and watch A.	Use reciprocal teaching when the children are copying the body shapes in the photographs so that they can help each other.
D Repeat the gallops in two's and finish in a circle.	
E Finish by falling asleep in the circle, gradually sink to the floor and copy some of the twitching, jerky movements performed by the dancer towards the close of the dance as he tries to settle down to sleep.	

Learning Outcomes

Children should be guided to:

- *Composing* – Respond spontaneously and improvise to the visual and aural stimuli showing a variety of movements.
- *Performing* – Isolate and use all body parts separately and in simple co-ordinations.
- *Appreciating* – Name all body parts and describe the movements they do with them. Suggest meanings in their actions and in the dance on video.

Music for the Dance

Recordings by the Penguin Café Orchestra, e.g. *Signs of Life* (see Audio Resources Appendix, page 85).

**VIDEO
TITLE**

The best of Gene Kelly. Singin' in the Rain

Director-Choreographers: Gene Kelly and Stanley Donan.
Released in 1952.

Synopsis

This musical parodies the moment in movie history when talkies took over from silent pictures. Despite many memorable dance sequences, the one that people always recall is the extract where Gene Kelly splashes in the puddles and the pouring rain, whilst dancing with his umbrella in front of a bewildered policeman.

Dance Ideas

The two ideas of dancing in the rain and puddles, and using an umbrella to dance with could be taken separately or combined in one framework.

Figure 4.15 Singin' in The Rain. © Bill Cooper.

Figure 4.16 Singin' in The Rain. © Bill Cooper.

Discussion and Video Analysis

Watch the *Singin' in the Rain* sequence and identify the movement content and how the umbrella is used. Describe the quality of movement which is mainly light and fluent, suggesting a care-free mood.

Ideas for Dance Frameworks and Choreographic Tasks

1. Walks, with a light-hearted easy feel.

   Change the direction of travel.

   Use different rhythm patterns.

2. Stretched body shapes, held in moments of stillness.

3. Learn the sideways travelling step where the feet cross over one another.

4. Learn the heel and toe step performed on the spot with each leg in turn.

5. From the dance in the puddles include

   (a) kicking the water

   (b) two-footed jumps into the puddle

   (c) pivoting on one leg and kicking the water with the other foot.

6. Dancing with the umbrella include:

   (a) Keeping it closed and swinging it, kicking with one foot onto a shoulder, holding it as if it were a dancing partner.

   (b) Open the umbrella and turn with it, turn it upside down and dance around it.

VIDEO TITLE | The Path

Synopsis

In this video the dancer/choreographer Carl Campbell presents his personal interpretation of Afro-Caribbean dance. He traces the influence of African dance on dance styles which have emerged from the West Indies and more recently American jazz dance. The dances are placed in an historical and cultural context as Carl explains their significance and demonstrates typical movement content. The Path is designed to depict how African movements emerge in our own time, illustrating the route blacks have travelled and how they have absorbed other dance forms.

When talking of dance in Africa Carl says: 'Dance is the culture, the culture expresses itself in dance... if you take away the dance you will be left with nothing.'

Dance Content (running order as on the video)

Section 1

Afro-Caribbean dance including (a) an explanation of the African and European influences and (b) a demonstration of the movement content.

Section 2

African dance including (a) a visual account of the significance of dance in every aspect of African life, (b) a demonstration of the dance style, and (c) a choreographed interpretation of African dance, including singing, drumming and masks.

Section 3

Caribbean dance including:

1. An account of how the African slaves developed their own dance style in the West Indies, making connections with religion and spiritualism, and highlighting the influence of European dance traditions, e.g. the samba.
2. A demonstration of the dance style.
3. A choreographed interpretation of Caribbean dance including carnival scenes.

Section 4

Jazz dance:

1. This opens with snippets of twentieth century western dance which developed with the advent of jazz music and includes the Charleston, Jitterbug, Jive, Rock 'n' Roll and Twist.
2. The influence of the people from the Caribbean on American jazz dance is explained.
3. Jazz dance is performed in a demonstration of the movement content and a short choreography.

Section 5

Disco dance of the 1980s concludes the video, with Afro-Caribbean influences made explicit.

African Dance

The features of this style include:
- Movement into the floor.
- A low centre of gravity, with bent knees and flat feet.
- Rhythmic patterns of movement.
- Isolation of body parts moving to different rhythms.

The music is traditionally played on a variety of drums and other percussion instruments.

Ideas for Dance Frameworks and Choreographic Tasks

A Warrior Dance

Watch the section on African dance:
1. Use claps, stamps, body percussion to create a strong rhythm pattern.
2. Running and jumping, holding clear powerful body shapes as though holding a spear and/or a shield.
3. In two's perform a non-contact 'mock' fight as a preparation for battle, include the ideas of moving over, under and around a partner.
4. Travelling steps including walks, stamps, jumps and hops.
5. Celebrating victory – creating a circle dance, moving in and out, across and around the circle, demonstrating physical skill and gestures of thanksgiving to the gods.

A Choreographic Interpretation of African or Caribbean Dance

Using movement content taken from the appropriate section of the video to provide suitable ideas:
1. Teach a movement motif in this style.
2. Ask the children to add one or two movements of their choice.
3. Perform the motifs as a whole class, in small groups, or in two's.
4. Use unison and canon to add variety.
5. Create different group patterns – e.g. circles, lines or wedges – to add visual interest.

A Dance Drama based in an African or Caribbean village

A narrative could be used where the everyday life of the people provides movement content for work actions e.g. harvesting, fishing, pounding grain, washing clothes. This could lead into a celebration dance using traditional movement content.

Music for the Dance

- African drumming – live or recorded, e.g. The Drummers of Burundi.
- Recordings by Hugh Masekela, Ladysmith Black Mambazo.
- Hurricane Zouk (see Audio Resources Appendix, page 85).

Tales of Beatrix Potter

Choreographed by Sir Frederick Ashton.

Premier. The film Tales of Beatrix Potter was released in 1971. The ballet was first danced by The Royal Ballet at the Royal Opera House on 4 December 1992.

Synopsis

Ashton has transferred the characters and stories of Beatrix Potter's tiny volumes to the screen to produce a full-scale ballet. Set amidst the beautiful Lake District countryside the dance recreates each animal with superb choreography to suit their personality and the tale.

The music is by John Lanchbery who based the score on Victorian and early Edwardian tunes that Beatrix Potter might herself have heard:

'Each animal has his or her own theme – a tarantella for Peter Rabbit, a waltz for the mice, a march for the pigs, a polka for Mr Jeremy Fisher, for example. These themes are woven into music that conveys the linking narrative."

(Royal Ballet Programme Notes)

Dance Content and Ideas

The work includes (running order as on the video):
- The Tale of Mrs Tiggy-Winkle who is seen gathering up her washing from the line (*see Framework*).
- A Mouse Waltz which could be used as an introduction to this dance style.
- Jemima Puddleduck and The Fox, in which Jemima is just saved from an untimely end.
- The Piglets Country Dance (*see Framework*).
- Pigling Bland's Dance which is technically very challenging for more experienced dancers.
- The Tale of Jeremy Fisher in which the frog goes fishing from his lily-pad boat (*see Framework*).
- Tale of the two Bad Mice who create havoc in the doll's house.
- Peter Rabbit joins the other characters at a picnic which develops into a country dance.
- Squirrel dance, in which Squirrel Nutkin is the central exuberant and mischievous figure.
- Finalé dance with many of the Beatrix Potter characters.

Discussion and Video Analysis

The following questions provide a structure for viewing which could be applied to *any* of the dances watched by the children. They should be encouraged to discuss and analyse what they have seen and could record their description and interpretation through words and pictures.
- What is the story being told in this dance?
- Who are the characters in the dance?
- How does the dance start and finish?
- How do you think the characters *feel*?
- Can you describe *what* the characters are doing? (Focus on action words such as travelling, jumping and turning.)

- *How* do the characters move? (Focus on the quality of movement such as quick, light, strong, bouncy.)
- Could you draw the (i) floor patterns, (ii) leg shapes?
- Which part of the dance stands out in your mind? Say why.
- Are some movements, steps or patterns repeated in the dance?
- How does the music sound? (Is it slow or fast, rhythmical, smooth or bouncy?)
- What particular sounds can you hear? (Such as tinkly, ringing, jangly)
- Do you think the music suits the movement? (Encourage explanations of the answer.)
- Did you enjoy the dance? Give at least three reasons for your answer (value personal opinions and preferences as well as evaluative comments).

Music for the Dance

- The original music is available on CD (see Audio Resources Appendix, page 85).
- Nineteenth-century ballet music would provide suitable accompaniment.
- Jeremy Fisher's dance can be performed to the 'Dance of the Reed Flutes' from the *Nutcracker Suite* by Tchaikovsky, or a similar polka tune.

Mrs Tiggy-Winkle's Washing Dance – A Solo Dance Framework for very young dancers

		Teaching points
A	Create a travelling sequence using some of the following steps, e.g. little runs, runs high and low, skips, include sways and turns on the spot. Whole class could perform any of the above in unison.	The task set could be very simple, e.g. use one travelling step, pause and turn on the spot – repeat or select two different travelling steps and include swaying and turning – repeat. The movement quality should be light and bouncy.
B	Teach a set study taken from Mrs T's arrival at the garden gate: 1. Half-turn to right and curtsy, half-turn to left and curtsy. 2. Feet together copy shuffle step, heels and toes, 4 x to the right, and back again. 3. Repeat (1) starting right to left. Repeat travel steps to an imaginary washing line.	Encourage the children to look carefully at what Mrs T does, note the changing directions and step pattern.
C	Using the literal action of 'taking in the washing' select from the following movement ideas and create a simple repetitive sequence: 1. Reaching high and dropping the washing into the basket, on the spot and/or travelling. 2. Include 'shaking' the clothes using the whole body, add jumps and turns. 3. Play 'hide and seek' in and out of the washing.	Emphasise the use of exaggerated actions which are repeated to make a rhythmical phrase and add extra actions so that the movement does not become mimetic.
D	Create a solo dance to 'show off' shoes using simple steps e.g. stretching feet to the front, side and behind, lifting feet up in different directions, travelling steps with legs lifted up behind (as on video).	This could be improvised to include various different steps.
E	Repeat Section B. Finish with a spinning turn holding the washing basket and end with a curtsy.	

Learning Outcomes

Children should be guided to:

- *Composing* – Compose action phrases, remember and repeat them.
- *Performing* – Control and co-ordinate their actions, improving the clarity and quality of the movement.
- *Appreciating* – Describe the dynamics and spatial patterns in the actions they perform and observe.

  NOTE: The dance could also be devised as a duet.

Piglets Country Dance – A Simple Dance Framework

Country dances traditionally use simple steps, different patterns/figures and are repetitive in structure and these elements would naturally suit this framework.

		Teaching points
A	Use a running step kicking the legs up at the back to dance on the spot and travel about the space, include turns. Meet a partner and travel together.	
B	A dance around B, and vice versa.	
C	Travel into a circle either a small group or whole class using a walk with feet pointed at the front or teach a step from the video, i.e. step R, L, stretch R foot and pause, repeat starting on the L.	Encourage spatial awareness and the ability to dance with a partner and as part of a group.
D	In the circle select some of the following ideas: 1. Use skips, runs and gallops to make different patterns and figures. 2. Move around and in and out of the circle. 3. 'All fall down' and shake legs in the air as on the video. This could be teacher directed or older children in groups of 4–8 could create their own circle dance.	Figures could include do-si-do, arming R and L, promenade and swing in two's, some of which may have been learnt previously in traditional set folk dances.

Learning Outcomes

Children should be guided to:

- *Composing* – Plan and compose sections of a folk dance using appropriate steps and patterns.
- *Performing* – Perform a range of simple dance steps and patterns with rhythmical awareness.
- *Appreciating* – Describe the overall structure of the dance and recognise the style of traditional country dance.

Figure 4.17
Jeremy Fisher's Dance.
© Bill Cooper.

Jeremy Fisher's Dance – A Simple Dance Framework

A Solo	Teaching points
A Teach a simple, repetitive series of knee bends (pliés) and foot stretches (tendues) which are performed in unison.	This is a preparation for jumping, stress well stretched feet and straight backs
B Create a short individual jumping motif which can be repeated, include different leg shapes as on the video and in Figures 4.17 and 4.18.	The children could draw the leg shapes and try to copy them. Note that some are symmetrical and others are asymmetrical shapes.
C Collect 'fishing tackle' and leap across the lily pads coming to rest on one lily pad.	This section might be improvised, but a clear finishing place is necessary
D Use repeated exaggerated gestures to represent fishing, then attempting to land the fish, struggle and finally fall into the water.	Emphasise the use of large, exaggerated gestures.
E Teach the section where Jeremy sits on the riverbank and flexes his right and left feet, stretches his legs and finally shakes his whole body.	The children can copy this from the video.
F Repeat B to finish.	

Learning Outcomes

Children should be guided to:
- *Composing* – Create a jumping pattern/phrase that can be repeated.
- *Performing* – Be able to jump with control and clarity of body shape.
- *Appreciating* – Describe and draw a variety of different types of jump.

Figure 4.18
Jeremy Fisher's Dance.
© Bill Cooper.

71

West Side Story

Choreographer – Jerome Robbins

Released in 1961

Synopsis

Adapted from a hugely successful stage show, this musical is a contemporary interpretation of Shakespeare's Romeo and Juliet. Set in New York, two rival gangs, the Sharks and the Jets, only meet when it is time for conflict or to 'rumble' on the city streets. When Tony, the ex-leader of the Jets, falls in love with Maria, the sister of the Sharks' leader, their relationship is doomed and ends in tragedy with Tony's death.

The choreography is based on jazz dance style and is particularly effective when it uses ensemble work to create powerful and hard-hitting images of gang warfare. The music by Leonard Bernstein with lyrics by Stephen Sondheim depicts the changing moods and feelings expressed in the work and at times has an almost operatic feel about it.

Dance Ideas

The main stimuli for dance are the notions of gang unity and conflict. The use of jazz dance as a style of movement to convey these ideas is one that can be clearly identified and copied.

Discussion and Video Analysis

Watch (a) the opening scene of the film in which the two gangs attempt to threaten and intimidate each other, and/or (b) the song 'Cool', set in an underground car park.

1. What is the main action content?

For example travelling steps, jumps, turns, kicks, and moments of stillness, whole body movements and isolated gestures.

2. How are the dancers moving?

For example fast, powerful, strong and athletic, contrasting with sections which are more fluent, smooth and sustained. With a clear sense of rhythm and use of syncopation.

3. What are the main features of jazz dance style?

● Sudden changes of action content and dynamics.
● Isolated gestures and moments of stillness, showing clear, precise body shapes.
● Contrast of movement which has a low centre of gravity and moves 'into' the floor with high jumps and an elevated body position.
● Body alignment which includes both 'turned in' and 'turned out' leg positions,
● Influence of the music to accompany rhythmic patterns and syncopated movement phrases.

4.   How is the mood created through the use of (a) movement and (b) group choreography?

For example:

(a)   Threatening gestures, the use of focus to intimidate and direct attention, aggressive explosive action phrases.

(b)   Performing in unison as a cohesive group to suggest unity, repetition of movement content to reinforce feelings, contrasting sections of movement to provide tension.

Ideas for Dance Frameworks and Choreographic Tasks

The dance could be performed in small groups of 6–8 dancers, larger groups or with the whole class, who would then be divided into two gangs.

Introduction

1. Individually walk about the space, set the mood through clicking fingers, use of focus and isolated gestures. Establish a whole group shape. *OR*

2. Two gangs start on stage in a clear group shape, use simple literal actions, e.g. playing cards, bouncing a basketball, smoking and drinking. *OR*

3. A leader from each gang starts on stage, dancers gradually enter and join their group. The two gangs set a dramatic scenario creating a feeling of pent-up aggression and tension.

Development Ideas

4. Travel towards each other using a simple step pattern of walks and clicking fingers.

Figure 4.19 West Side Story. © Bill Cooper.

5. Create a duet with a member of the opposite gang to convey hostility. Movement content could include:
   – actions: jump, reach, drop, kick, turn, isolations
   – dynamics: stillness, sudden and sustained
   – space: over, under and around.
   Use focus to enhance the dramatic intention. This could be developed into a group fight scene.

6. Using specific movement content from the video – e.g. travel steps, jumps with clear body shapes, turning jumps, reaches and kicks – create a motif which demonstrates group unity (Figures 4.19 and 4.20). This could be performed separately by each gang while the other group observe disdainfully.

7. Teach a set study using jazz dance movement content.

Music for the Dance

- The original film soundtrack (see Audio Resources Appendix, page 85).
- Contemporary jazz music for the set study, e.g. Jools Holland, Bruce Hornsby.

Figure 4.20 West Side Story. © Bill Cooper.

Where Angels Fear to Tread

This video would be most suitable for students studying dance at Key Stage 4, GCSE and 'A'-level.

Choreographers – Mark Murphy, artistic director of V-TOL Dance Company (Vertical Take-off and Landing) and the performers, 25 BTEC and 'A'-level students of dance, performing arts and music.

Premier – The site was the Union Chapel in Islington, London, which was used to create a large-scale site-specific promenade work which received six public performances in 1995.

Synopsis

Background Context

The video is the outcome of an education project involving students from City and Islington College in London working with V-TOL's Artistic Director Mark Murphy, a composer, a designer, and V-TOL company dancers over an intensive 4-week period. It was designed as a promenade performance set in a Gothic chapel and incorporates original choreography, text and a live music score. The site-specific nature of the choreography involved both dancers, musicians and the audience moving about the chapel throughout the performances:

> 'On the evening the Union Chapel resembled a building site but although building work was a reality it was used skilfully and it blended imperceptibly into a context and an environment which the audience explored. From the first scenes of tender, frozen embraces the atmosphere was electric. As the observers continued their journey into the depths of the building the performers led us through layer after layer of human interaction, all simmering with covert drama.'
>
> (Professor Christopher Bannerman, The Union Chapel Project, V-TOL Dance Company, November 1995)

Mark Murphy formed V-TOL in 1991 and the company strives to challenge traditional concepts of dance, integrating movement with other mediums and reflecting influences which include film, visual art, literature and popular music. Their work is characterised by its concern with issues in contemporary society and a need to communicate intense human emotion through a powerful movement vocabulary:

> 'V-TOL's movement style is full of raw energy and hovers on the brink between high-speed, almost dangerous athleticism and moments of extreme tenderness.'
>
> (*History of the Company* – education notes)

When discussing the physical style he has developed Mark Murphy explains it as coming 'from me trying to form a conduit from what I feel and what I do physically'.

The Dance Idea

In this project the stimuli given to the performers were the different ways in which people are hurt emotionally. The ideas that arose out of discussing and brainstorming those situations generated a list of starting points for movement exploration. Mark Murphy describes one method they employed:

> 'We did work on things you wish you could say to people but have never had the opportunity or the guts or the chance to say, so they went away and wrote down lots of things.'   (Interview notes)

He started from well-known experiences that the performers could recognise and tap into such as living in a confined space with someone, or people trying to leave each other and the notions of guilt and innocence which result from certain situations in life. The movement is intrinsically linked to these emotional starting points creating a dynamic vocabulary through which the performers communicate the ideas.

The students were encouraged to develop their own creative skills and individual artistic language, involving a democratic process which gave them an equal responsibility for the material developed and the final 20 minute piece. The working approach was structured to provide the students with the experience of participating as members of a professional company.

The Music

The original intention was to have live music, created by music students who worked with the dancers. In the event the students were made up of a group with very different musical experiences and skills, including 2 drama students who both played instruments and an injured dancer. Dominic Murcott, the composer, found this a challenging task and decided:

> 'The first thing that we had to do was find a group language, "This is our band – what do we sound like, what can we do"?'
> (Interview notes)

The musicians were involved throughout the project and worked closely with the dancers. Dominic Murcott explains,

> 'As for the music and dance working together, I think we worked on things separately, making music not for any particular section, but as I said before finding out what sounds we can make. Then we would look at something the dancers had been working on...'
> (Interview notes)

They were also an integral part of the dance work, being on stage and on view during the performance.

Dance Content (running order as on the video)

All the quotes are taken from an interview given by Mark Murphy and Dominic Murcott to Professor Christopher Bannerman (November 1995).

Section 1: A surreal ballroom scene

This involves the whole group:

> 'It was based in a strange sort of social dance where people will just kind of flip...'
> '...we wanted a canon of people leaving each other, which was one of the ways of hurting people we explored.'
> '...in the end they help their partners to sleep very tenderly, waited until they were asleep and sneaked away.'

Section 2: The ID Parade

> '...This comes from the idea that in an ID parade there may be one guilty person in a whole line of non-guilty people or maybe they're all not guilty or all guilty even.'

Section 3: The Balcony

There are three cubicles on the balcony with one wall removed to allow the audience to see what is happening in each separate space:

'...the cubicles were derivative of living side by side with people or living in close proximity to each other.'

Section 4: The Cellar

This depicts the darker aspects of life, a trapped environment with little hope for the future:

'...it was a bit of a prison, a mental prison..... they realised that this was a dead end for them, that they had to go somewhere else.'

Section 5: The Chapel

'...the chapel was about finally getting things off their chests... to purge themselves... they had the possibility to start piecing things back together again.'

The dance concludes with one dancer saying 'I need you' which the performers use to indicate that we are all social beings, dependent to a certain extent on other people. As Mark Murphy suggests: 'It almost starts another piece, "I need you but where do we go from here?"'

Discussion and Video Analysis

View Section 1, the 'ballroom' scene

- How might you describe the two contrasting moods depicted during this section? For example:
  - (i) Initially each couple is supportive, harmonious and literally 'in touch' with each other; this contrasts with
  - (ii) A frenzied and angry feeling which tears the dancers apart.
- How does the movement content communicate these emotional ideas? For example:
  - (i) At first the couples are in close physical contact performing gentle swaying movements, smooth opening and closing action phrases, sustained lifts and supports.
  - (ii) In contrast they then separate and move in a strong sudden, jerky style, one dancer on the floor supporting their weight with different body parts and the other using powerful gestures and clear, angular body shapes.

Refer to Figures 4.21 and 4.22 to illustrate the change in feeling between the two dancers and how this is shown in the body shapes and relationships.

- What might be the reasons for this change? Are there times in life when things seem to be going smoothly and then the unexpected happens? What might cause the couples to react in this way to each other?
- The dancers perform a motif in unison, what feelings does this suggest? For example, acting as individuals within a group, identity with others but standing alone.
- At the end of this section the dancers leave their partner lying on the floor, eventually everyone leaves the space. What meaning might this convey? For example, loneliness, rejection, guilt.

Figure 4.21 *Where Angels Fear to Tread.*
© Andrew Lang.

Figure 4.22 *Where Angels Fear to Tread.*
© Andrew Lang.

View Section 3, the 'balcony' scene

● How might you describe the range of feelings conveyed in each of the 'cubicle' scenes? For example, in each of them there is a contrast between tender, caring moments and an aggressive, violent mood.

● How does the use of a confined space contribute to the emotional ideas? For example, feeling trapped, unable to have your own personal space, living in close contact with another person and the pressures that can arise.

● How does the movement content communicate these ideas? Does each 'cubicle' dance suggest a range of different feelings? For example:

(i) The first duet – this starts with simple gestures touching a partner's face to suggest tenderness and warmth. These become more violent and develop into striking actions; the duet involves pushing, pulling, throwing and hugging a partner, with focus being used to create tension; the mood changes quickly to and fro between love and affection, and anger and frustration.

(ii) The trio – this uses a series of simple repetitive gestures performed in unison to give a mechanistic and emotionless feel to start their dance.

(iii) The middle duet uses two dancers who appear to manipulate each other as they fling their partner about the space, they also react to external forces which seem to wrack their bodies.

● How is the overall visual design of this section shaped to allow each duet or trio to be seen

whilst interrelating it with the other dancers? For example, one group performs whilst the other two are either still or moving minimally, groups use the same movement style and sometime echo each other's movements, there are short bursts of movement from each group in turn.

The Complete Dance

What are the stylistic features of this work which are often associated with 'New dance' or 'Post-modern dance'? For example, the dance:

1. Does not employ a strict dance technique.

2. Uses everyday movement.

3. Involves manipulation of props, acting and musicians who are integral to the choreography.

4. Does not have an obvious storyline or logical progression.

5. Allows dancers to take on different characters.

6. Includes dancing which is disrupted by other kinds of activity.

Comparisons could be made with *'Flesh and Blood'* choreographed by Lea Anderson for The Cholmondeleys.

Ideas for Dance Frameworks and Choreographic Tasks

The following movement ideas could be used to explore and create material which could then be ordered to communicate a storyline, convey an emotional context or express changing relationships. The students and the teacher could collaboratively devise a framework which reflects the episodic structure of the original choreography.

With Reference to Section 1

Movement Ideas

In each instance students should be encouraged to explore fully the potential movement content associated with the stimulus or idea.

1. In two's create a movement phrase that suggests harmony and togetherness. Use ideas from the video, including:

    (a) the traditional ballroom hold and simple steps,

    (b) opening and closing moves between the two dancers,

    (c) gentle swaying movements in contact with each other,

    (d) sustained lifts and supports – use Figure 4.22 to copy a supported position.

2. Working individually create a movement phrase which conveys feelings of conflict, discord, anger etc. Use ideas from the video, including:

    (a) working on the floor, supporting the body weight on different parts such as hands and feet,

    (b) standing and using strong, powerful gestures,

(c) use of clear body shapes and held angular positions,

(d) a change of level.

Use Figure 4.21 to demonstrate these ideas.

3. In two's create a duet sequence which uses the movement material from (2). This could include choreographic devices such as,

(a) action and reaction,

(b) contrasting and complementary,

(c) question and answer.

4. As a group learn a motif which uses movement material from (2). Perform in unison, or half the group dance whilst their partner remains still and vice versa.

5. Explore ways of leaving your partner, the movement content should reflect the emotional idea. For example:

● creeping away whilst they are asleep,

● running from them as they watch you go,

● leaving reluctantly but having to go,

● tearing apart from each other,

● realising they have gone and chasing after them.

With Reference to Section 3

The dancers could work in two's or three's to create a piece which conveys the idea of being in a relationship forced to exist in a relatively small space. This space could literally be physically small but could also symbolise the enclosed mental space that these individuals are required to operate and live within. These dances could be juxtaposed beside one or two other groups so that the choreography suggests the different human relationships that exist side by side.

Movement Ideas

● Learn the opening phrase of movement in the 1st duet where the dancers gently touch each other's faces in turn. Refer to Figure 4.24. Develop this idea through, for example, enlarging the gestures, adding action content, changing the dynamics.

● Use a bank of action words to stimulate improvisation, leading to the creation of a movement motif which communicates the constantly changing mood of the first duet, e.g. pull, push, dive, throw, drop, hug, cling, turn, look, stare. Use ideas from the video and restrict the amount of floor space and distance between the two dancers.

● With reference to the trio explore gestures which can be made into a repetitive pattern. This could be used to convey a lack of emotion and provide a contrast to other sections.

● Use ideas from the middle duet to explore:

(a) *the feeling of manipulation,* e.g. involve moving a partner about the space using physical contact and reacting to unseen external forces which exert influences on each dancer's body, hurling them across the room.

(b) *the illusion of being trapped inside a space,* e.g. using rebound and striking movements to communicate this idea and moments of stillness and sustained actions to provide contrasting dynamics.

Figures 4.23 and 4.24 *Where Angels Fear to Tread* © Andrew Lang.

Figure 4.24

● Choreograph a piece which uses two or three groups performing their dance together and redesign elements in time so that the whole work has a sense of unity. This may involve the duets or trios stopping and starting at different times, holding moments of stillness and repeating sections. Refer to Figure 4.23 and discuss how this section is designed on the video.

Note

The style of movement involved in this dance includes moments of physical challenge and risk taking. This is an exciting and demanding way of creating movement and working with others, and teachers should be aware of the *safety procedures* which need to be considered by themselves and the students. These should include:

1. An appropriate and thorough warm-up. Trainers may be worn, particularly on non-sprung floors.
2. Sensitivity and trust when working together. This will take time and a carefully considered teaching approach.
3. Adequate supervision of work in progress.
4. Careful rehearsal of the choreography.

Music for the dance

The original music is available on tape in the resources pack.

DANCE FOR THE CAMERA – OUTSIDE IN

This 15 minute work is performed by CandoCo, a company of six dancers, three of whom are physically disabled. The dancers' bodies and their wheelchairs are used to create a witty and visually striking choreography described as a voyage of discovery and surprises.

DANCEHOUSE

The video contains a series of 12 5-minute dance films made especially for the screen and designed to reflect a range of styles in modern dance. This 1990 production for BBC TV and the Arts Council includes a version of *Cinderella* set to Latin rhythms; an Oriental duet; a Kathak solo without the traditional Indian costume and setting and a high-energy work inspired by dance in London nightclubs.

Choreographers include: Kim Brandstrup, Aletta Collins, Gary Lambert, Jacob Marley.

DANCE INTO SCHOOLS – THE JIVING LINDY HOPPERS

Synopsis

In this video demonstration the company of five dancers give a performance of dances of the 1930s and 1940s including the Lindy Hop and the Big Apple. They also work with a class of 9-10-year-old school children, teaching them the basic steps, discussing the stylistic features and also how the dance relates to the jazz music of this era.

Dance Content

● A performance of the Big Apple by the three women and two men in the company.
● Two members of the company work with children, demonstrating and teaching set steps such as the 'Stomp Off', 'Susie Q' and 'Charleston'.
● A final performance showing the Big Apple and Lindy Hop danced by the company.

Dance Ideas

● Many of the basic steps are quite simple and could be used to teach a set study. The children could work individually, with a partner and in small groups.
● Having watched the video and discussed the style the children could create their own simple movement patterns. They might copy a step that is on the spot and then turn, travel sideways, forwards and backwards, adding their own arm and leg gestures.
● Some of the partner work could be learnt and adapted from the video, including simple lifts. These movement later evolved into the jive and eventually rock 'n' roll dance.

TAP DOGS

This all-male Australian dance group present a dazzling display of tap-dancing. The six men who wear jeans, shorts and checkshirts are bursting with energy. To the accompaniment of driving rhythms they dance up and down ramps, scale ladders and perform in water wearing wellingtons. The live recording is full of dynamism, invention and humour.

DIFFERENT STEPS

A view of three different approaches to choreography by Rambert's principal choreographers of the 1980s. The video features extracts from:

- *Wildlife* by Richard Alston.
- *Sergeant Early's Dream* by Christopher Bruce.
- *Death and the Maiden* by Robert North.

There are also teachers' notes and an audio cassette available.

NEVER AGAIN

By DV8 Physical Dance Theatre. This contemporary dance deals with attitudes towards homosexuality in our society. The movement content is very powerful and uses physical contact to convey the changing relationships depicted in the work. It is filmed on location and makes very striking use of set design and visual effects in the recording.

FOUR BY KYLIAN

An anthology of modern ballets choreographed by Jiri Kylian and performed by The Nederlands Dans Theater.

Synopsis

This video features four works by the Czechoslovakian Jiri Kylian, who is one of today's leading international choreographers:

- *Svadebka* (Les Noces) – This interpretation of Stravinsky's peasant wedding story to the scores Les Noces is 'memorable for its earthliness and humour' (Vision Video Ltd., 1992).
- *La Cathédrale Engloutie* – Performed to music by Debussy, this work is inspired by a fifteenth-century Breton legend and tells of a cathedral which crumbled into the sea when the people led sinful lives.
- *Sinfonietta* – This work is the company's signature piece, set to Janáck's score it is an exuberant ballet of life's joys and sorrows.
- *Torso* – Dedicated to the world's émigrés, it is danced to music by the Japanese composer Toru Takemitsu.

RIVERDANCE

Taken from the enormously successful theatre production, this video draws on an eclectic range of dance traditions to provide an entertaining look at dance. Traditional Irish dancers and musicians feature most strongly, demonstrating the technical skills required in this folk style and extending them to create a new movement vocabulary and a fusion of musical influences.

THAT'S DANCING

Synopsis

This video charts the story of dance on film and includes a range of dance styles performed by key figures in the history of dance on film in the twentieth century. The many extracts are quite short but provide an image of dance in each era.

Dance Content

This includes sections of:
● Breakdancing.
● Early C20 musicals, showing the Charleston and featuring several spectacular Busby Berkeley shows.
● Fred Astaire and Ginger Rogers.
● Tap dancers including Shirley Temple, Bill 'Bojangles' Robinson and the amazing Nicholas Brothers.
● A scene from the *Wizard of Oz* with the Strawman.
● Dance artists including Isadora Duncan and Anna Pavlova.
● Gene Kelly dancing with cartoon figures and dustbin lids.
● Broadway musicals such as *Oklahoma* and *Sweet Charity*.
● Modern musicals such as *West Side Story, Saturday Night Fever, Fame, Flashdance,* and Michael Jackson performing '*Beat It*'.

Dance Ideas

The range of different dance styles included on this video could provide valuable starting points for choreography which reflect their essential characteristic elements. It also provides historical material which places dance in a context and would enhance children's appreciation of the development of certain types of dance during the twentieth century.

5   Appendices

Appendix 1/Audio Resources

Tape *A Gift of Tradition* produced by SAMPAD
      Classical South Asian music
Tape *Batucada* Escola de Mociade Independente de Padre Miguel   JSL 003 1520
Tape *Hurricane Zouk* Various Artists   Virgin TCEWV2
CD   *Incantation* with the Sergeant Early Band:
      – Sergeant Early's Dream
      – Ghost Dances   COOK CD69
Tape *Late Flowering Love* John Betjeman   EMI VCC MC21
Tape *Signs of Life* Penguin Café Orchestra   Virgin
CD   Original Soundtrack Recording, Orchestra of the Royal Opera House, EMI Classics
      Tales of Beatrix Potter – by John Lanchbery   7545372
Tape *Timbalada* Cada Cabece and Um Mondo   Polygram 522813-2
Tape *Walking the Circle* by Inner Sense   Hula 003
      Inner sense produce several percussion tapes, and a newsletter, contact
      Inner Sense, The Croft, Old Church Road, Colwall, Worcs WR13 6EZ
CD   Original Soundtrack Recording
      West Side Story by Leonard Bernstein   CBS 4676062

Appendix 2/Video Resources

For addresses and telephone numbers see Useful Addresses (page 86)
An Evening with the Rambert Dance Company – Polygram £15.50   079 277 3
      Intimate Pages
      Lonely Town Lonely Street
      Sergeant Early's Dream
Dancehouse – Dancclincs Production   £50
Available from Concord Video Film Council.
Dance Into Schools: Unit B – The Jiving Lindy Hoppers – £35 plus p&p plus VAT
      Educational Media, Film and Video Ltd.
Dance Theatre of Harlem – Polygram £15.99   079 2373
      Fall River Legend
      Troy Game
      The Beloved
      John Henry

Dein Perry's Tap Dogs – PG Warner Vision – £10.99
Different Steps – A view of three different approaches to choreography – £29 video, £35 with
    notes and audio cassette. Available from Alison Whyte, Education Manager, Rambert
    Dance Company
Four By Kylian – Polygram – £15.50   079 286 3
Gift of Tradition – A documentary on South Asian Dance – £20
    Available from Sampad
Houston Ballet – Dance Videos £15.99   DV9
    Ghost Dances
    Image
    Journey
Kathak Dance – Educational Media, Film and Video Ltd. – £29.50
Late Flowering Lust – BBC £10.99   BBCV 5252
L'Enfant et Les Sortilèges – Polygram – £15.50   079 257 3
Never Again – DV8 Physical Dance Theatre, Dance Videos £15.99
Anarkos – danced by Random Dance Co., see Spring Re-Loaded, available from
  The Video Place £12.50
Riverdance – The Show, Video Collection – £13.99   VC 6494
Still Life at the Penguin Café – Decca – £15.50   071 122 3
That's Dancing – MGM – £10.99   SO 50613
The Best of Gene Kelly – Castle Communications – £10.99   CV1 4251
The Path – Educational Media Film and Video Ltd. – £29.50
The Tales of Beatrix Potter – The Royal Ballet, Warner £10.99   PES 38026
West Side Story – MGM/UA £10.99   SO 99244
Where Angels Fear to Tread – V-TOL Dance Company – £37.65

Appendix 3/Useful Publications

A Directory of Resources for Dance Teaching edited by Rachel Lightfoot, published by
Contemporary Dance Trust (1995). Available from Education and Community Programmes
Department, The Place, 17 Dukes Road, London WC1H 9AB. Tel. 0171 388 8956
Music of Brazil (1997) Naughton, C. and Seddon, C., WOMAD.

Appendix 4/Useful Addresses

ADiTi. 46–47 Chancery Lane, London WC2

Arts Council Film and Video Library. This has a considerable number of dance works on
video, some of which may be purchased and others which are only available on hire. These
include the programmes shown on the BBC2 series 'Dance for the Camera' which display
very diverse styles of dance. For details contact: **Concord Video Film Council**, 201
Felixstowe Road, Ipswich, Suffolk IP3 9BJ. Tel. 01473 726012

Dance Books. This is one of the world's largest specialist dance bookshops. Their stock
includes many of the videos mentioned in this text as well as books, magazines, tapes,

compact discs and many piano scores. They provide a comprehensive retail catalogue on request from: 15 Cecil Court, St Martin's Lane, London WC2N 4EZ. Tel. 0171 836 2314, Fax 0171 497 0473.

Dance UK. An independent, non profit-making organisation for all forms of professional dance, it publishes a quarterly magazine and various information sheets. 23 Crisp Road, London W6 9RL. Tel. 0181 741 1932, Fax 0181 748 0186.

Educational Media, Film and Video Ltd. – Tel. 0181 868 1908.

National Dance Teachers Association (NDTA). This voluntary organisation is concerned with dance in schools and publishes a termly magazine, *Dance Matters*. It is shortly to produce a resource list of materials available to support the teaching of dance in schools. For further information and membership details contact: Carolyn Woolridge, Treasurer NDTA, 29 Larkspur Avenue, Burntwood, Staffs WS7 8FR.

National Resource Centre for Dance (NRCD). Based at the University of Surrey the centre contains a wide range of dance publications, including videos, and offers research services. A catalogue of NRCD publications is available from: The Secretary (Publications), National Resource Centre for Dance, University of Surrey, Guildford, Surrey GU2 5XH. Tel. 01483 259316, Fax 01483 300803.

Rambert Dance Company – 94 Chiswick High Road, London W4 1SH

SAMPAD. c/o Mac, Cannon Hill Park, Birmingham B12 9QH. Tel. 0121 440 4221, Fax 0121 440 8667.

The Video Place. Based at The Place Theatre, which is part of The Contemporary Dance Trust, they have a catalogue of videos available from 2 Spring Re-Loaded dance seasons. The 16 videos each feature recordings of a live performance and include an interview with the choreographer. A preview tape of the work is available. Companies include: Random Dance Company, Yolande Smith Theatredance and Motionhouse Dance Theatre. The Video Place, 17 Dukes Road, London WC1H 9AB. Tel. 0171 383 0516.

V-TOL Dance Company – 92/94 Judd Street, London WC1H 9NT. Tel. 0171 278 2432.

Appendix 5/Children's thoughts on the use of professional dance on video

Having watched the video *A Gift of Tradition* and used it to help create a South Asian dance, a class of Year 4 children were given an evaluation worksheet.

The four questions, together with some of their responses, are included to demonstrate the type and range of learning which took place.

1. Did you enjoy the video? If so can you say why?
- I liked the music, the rhythms are good.
- It made me happy and I really liked dancing like they did.
- It was interesting and enjoyable, the costumes were great, so was the beat.

2. What can you remember about the video?
- The different styles, the temple dance and shiva.
- The screen went red and people were fighting with swords.
- I liked the musical instrument sounds.

3. How did you use what you saw on the video in your dance lesson?
- We copied the shapes.
- We did a lot of jumping like the bhangra people did.
- I used the feet movement and the rhythms and some of the gestures.

4. Do you think what you saw on the video has helped you learn more about dance? If so can you say how?
- It helped my memory.
- It built up my confidence.
- It's a different culture to ours in the West, we have Maypole and Morris dancing, they have bhangra and temple dancing.
- It has given me better ideas for dance lessons.

BIBLIOGRAPHY

Arts Council (1993) *Dance in Schools.* London: Arts Council of Great Britain.
Bacon, L. (1974) *A Handbook of Morris Dancing.*
Best, D. (1992) *The Rationality of Feeling.* Lewes: Falmer Press.
Ellfeldt, L. (1974) *A Primer for Choreographers.* London: Dance Books.
Harlow, M. and Rolfe, L. (1992) *Let's Dance: a Handbook for Teachers.* London: BBC.
Mackrell, J. (1992) *Out of Line – The Story of British New Dance.* London: Dance Books.
OFSTED (1995) *Framework for Inspection.* London: HMSO.
Peck, A. (1978) *The Morris and Sword Dances of England.* Hertfordshire: Hive Printers Ltd.
Robertson, A. and Hutera, D. (1988) *The Dance Handbook.* Harlow: Longman.
Smith-Autard, J. (1994) *The Art of Dance in Education.* London: A.&C. Black.
Swanwick, K. (1994) *Musical Knowledge: Intuition, Analysis and Music Education.* London: Routledge.